Remaking Domestic Intelligence

*The Hoover Institution
gratefully acknowledges
the generous support of*

JERONIMO *and* JAVIER ARANGO

on this publication.

Remaking Domestic Intelligence

Richard A. Posner

HOOVER INSTITUTION PRESS
Stanford University   Stanford, California

www.hoover.org

Hoover Institution Press Publication No. 541

First printing, 2005
12   11   10   09   08   07   06   05   9   8   7   6   5   4   3   2   1

Manufactured in the United States of America

The paper used in this publication meets the minimum requirements of the American National Standard for Information Sciences— Permanence of Paper for Printed Library Materials, ANSI Z39.48-1992. ∞

Library of Congress Cataloging-in-Publication Data
Remaking domestic intelligence / by Richard A. Posner.
        p.   cm. — (Hoover Institution Press publication ; no. 541)
    ISBN 0-8179-4682-9 (alk. paper)
    1. Intelligence service—United States.   2. Canadian Security Intelligence
Service.   I. Title.   II. Series.
JK468.I6P672   2006
363.25'0973—dc22   2005020467

Contents

Prefatory Note

The magnitude of the terrorist threat to the United States, coupled with the lack of coordination among our domestic intelligence agencies and the continuing failure of the lead agency, the Federal Bureau of Investigation, to develop an adequate domestic intelligence capability, argues compellingly for reform. This monograph by Richard A. Posner, a federal circuit judge and a senior lecturer at the University of Chicago Law School, and the author of *Preventing Surprise Attacks: Intelligence Reform in the Wake of 9/11* (2005), develops the case for reform and makes concrete proposals.

Because the FBI's failure is systemic, being rooted in the incompatibility of criminal law enforcement (the FBI's principal mission) with national security intelligence, the reform must have a structural dimension. Under pressure from the White House, the FBI has now reluctantly agreed to create a unit to be called the "National Security Service," by fusing the Bureau's three divisions that at present share intelligence responsibility. This reorganization may or may not be a good idea; but clearly it is not enough. The Director of National Intelligence should take the coordination and command of domestic intelligence firmly into his hands by appointing a deputy for domestic intelligence. Even more important, a true domestic intelligence agency—which is to say an agency that like England's MI5 or the Canadian Security Intelligence Service would have no law enforcement functions—should be created and lodged in the Department of Homeland Security. Intelligence fits better into an agency concerned with preventing attacks than into one concerned with prosecuting the attackers. The reorganization of DHS announced by Secretary Michael Chertoff on July 13, 2005, is potentially a first step toward the creation of a U.S. Security Intelligence Service.

This monograph borrows some material from chapter 6 of *Preventing Surprise Attacks* but is mainly new. The author thanks Lindsey Briggs, Paul Clark, Raina Kim, and Meghan Maloney for exemplary research assistance, and Stewart Baker, Scott Hemphill, Grace Mastalli, Ted Price, Laurence Silberman, George Spix, Thomas Twetten, and James Q. Wilson for valuable advice and stimulating comments. The extensive comments of Baker, Spix, and Twetten on successive drafts deserve a special acknowledgment. Remaining errors are the author's own.

July 20, 2005

1. The Problem

Introduction

"Domestic national security intelligence" ("domestic intelligence" for short) is intelligence concerning threats of major, politically motivated violence, or of equally grievous harm to national security, mounted within the nation's territorial limits, whether by international terrorists, homegrown terrorists, or spies or saboteurs employed by foreign nations. The 9/11 attacks reflected a failure of domestic intelligence, having been mounted from within the United States by terrorists who had been in this country for months—some intermittently for years.

The danger of terrorist acts committed on the soil of the United States has not abated despite strenuous efforts to improve homeland security. The hostility of significant segments of the vast Muslim world (including large and restive Muslim minorities in such European nations as the United Kingdom, France, and the Netherlands) toward the United States is unabated. And weapons of mass destruction—atomic bombs, dirty bombs (conventional explosives that scatter radioactive material), chemical agents, lethal pathogens, and deadly-when-abused industrial materials—are ever cheaper and more available. Their cost will continue to decline, and their availability to increase, faster than the defensive measures planned or deployed at present.[1] Nor can

1. On the threat to U.S. national security posed by weapons of mass destruction in the hands of terrorists, see Richard A. Posner, *Catastrophe: Risk and Response* 71–86 (2004), and references cited there.

it be assumed that the threat of terrorism with weapons of mass destruction comes only from the Muslim world, or indeed only from foreign groups or nations. The Unabomber, Timothy McVeigh, the FALN (a violent Puerto Rican separatist organization), the Weather Underground, and the Black Panthers are historical examples of homegrown U.S. terrorists whose successors may wield enormously greater lethal power.

It is difficult to imagine any major attack on the United States (other than by an enemy nation) that would not have a domestic aspect. Even an attack that consisted of exploding a ship full of ammonium nitrate (or carrying a dirty bomb or a nuclear bomb) in a U.S. port would take place within the defensive perimeter of the Coast Guard, whose intelligence service is a part of the federal intelligence community, and would undoubtedly have been prepared with the help of people living in the United States, if only because the attackers would need information about port security.

The meaningfulness of "domestic intelligence" as a category might be questioned on the ground that borders have no significance when the main threat to national security comes from international terrorism. Certainly domestic and foreign intelligence must be closely coordinated. But there are enough differences to justify preserving the distinction. Domestic intelligence presents civil liberties concerns that are absent or attenuated when intelligence agencies operate abroad, since the Constitution and laws of the United States generally do not have extraterritorial application. And homegrown terrorists—terrorists with no personal, familial, ethnic, or political ties to a foreign country—are a major potential threat in an era of weapons of mass destruction. Recruitment, training, deployment, and security requirements are also different for intelligence officers operating inside and outside national borders. Surveillance methods are apt to differ too. And domestic intelligence officers must work closely with the nation's public and private police and protection forces to create a nationwide network of eyes and ears.

Despite its importance to national security, domestic intelligence is the weakest link in the U.S. intelligence system. The proximate cause is the entrustment of domestic intelligence to the FBI; a more remote cause is that Americans tend to disregard foreign experience. The final report of the National Commission on Terrorist Attacks Upon the United States (the 9/11 Commission) cast only a cursory glance at foreign intelligence systems, even though some of them, notably the British, French, and Israeli, are well regarded. These are also nations that have a longer experience dealing with terrorism than the United States. Each has a domestic intelligence agency that is separate from its national police force, its counterpart to the FBI, and has no power of arrest or other law enforcement powers. In Britain the domestic intelligence agency is called the Security Service, better known as MI5; in France, the Direction de la Surveillance du Territoire (DST); in Israel, Shin Bet. Examples of similar agencies in other nations are the Bundesamt für Verfassungsschutz (BfV) in Germany, the Public Security Investigation Agency in Japan, the Australian Security Intelligence Organisation, the New Zealand Security Intelligence Service, the Intelligence Bureau in India, the National Intelligence Agency in South Africa, and—an agency that I shall especially emphasize as a possible model for a U.S. domestic intelligence agency—the Canadian Security Intelligence Service.[2] There is an international

2. On the various foreign domestic intelligence agencies, see Michael A. Turner, *Why Secret Intelligence Fails*, ch. 4 (2005); Peter Chalk and William Rosenau, *Confronting the 'Enemy Within': Security Intelligence, the Police, and Counterterrorism in Four Democracies* (RAND Corp. 2004); Todd Masse, "Domestic Intelligence in the United Kingdom: Applicability of the MI-5 Model to the United States: Report for Congress" (Congressional Research Service, Order Code RL31920, May 19, 2003). Some of the agencies, though not the British or Canadian, have ancillary law enforcement responsibilities. And some nations, such as

consensus that a nation's intelligence system should include a domestic intelligence capability that is separate from the police. The consensus includes the nations of "old Europe" admired by American liberals who are in the forefront of opposition to emulating the European approach to domestic security.

Although the United States is an outlier in not having such an agency, the 9/11 Commission gave the back of its hand[3] to proposals[4] that we create one. Members and staff of the commission visited the director-general of MI5, who told them she "doubt[ed] that such an agency could operate under the restrictions of the U.S. Constitution and the traditionally higher American emphasis on civil liberties and the right to privacy. 'Even the Brits think it wouldn't work here,' 9/11 Commission Chairman Thomas Kean said in a news conference shortly after the

---

Italy and Spain, combine foreign and domestic intelligence; the Italian agency is the Servizio per la Informazioni e la Sicurezza Democratica (SISDE) and the Spanish agency is the Centro Nacional de Inteligencia (CNI). For an extensive list of the world's intelligence agencies, see www.globalsecurity.org/intell/world/india/index.html.

3. *Final Report of the National Commission on Terrorist Attacks Upon the United States* 423–424 (July 2004).

4. See, for example, *Protecting America's Freedom in the Information Age: A Report of the Markle Foundation Task Force*, Oct. 2002, http://markletaskforce.org/documents/Markle_Full_Report.pdf; William E. Odom, *Fixing Intelligence: For a More Secure America*, ch. 8 (2003); Odom, "Why the FBI Can't Be Reformed," *Washington Post*, June 29, 2005, p. A21; John Deutch, "Strengthening U.S. Intelligence," testimony before the 9/11 Commission, Oct. 14, 2003, at www.9-11commission.gov/hearings/hearing4/witness_deutch.htm; Paul R. Pillar, "Intelligence," in *Attacking Terrorism: Elements of a Grand Strategy* 115, 133–134 (Audrey Kurth Cronin and James M. Ludes, eds., 2004); William Rosenau and Peter Chalk, "Can We Learn from Others?" *Wall Street Journal*, Apr. 15, 2004, p. A14. In 2003, Senator John Edwards made a proposal for a domestic intelligence agency that is similar to the proposal in this monograph; his proposal is described in Fayza Elmostehi and Michael D. Vozzo, "Domestic Intelligence and National Security Reform Proposals," 2004, www.maxwell.syr.edu/campbell/Library%20Papers/Event%20papers/ISHS/ElmoStehiVozzo.pdf. See also the statement by Senator Richard Shelby, note 14 below, from which I shall be quoting extensively.

commission issued its report."[5] To defer to the opinion of a foreign official concerning the limits that U.S. law and custom would place on a domestic intelligence service makes little sense—and anyway all that the director-general may have meant was that a U.S. service couldn't be a carbon copy of her agency because the legal framework would be different. It does not follow that the difference (which is anyway slight now that the United Kingdom has signed the European Convention on Human Rights) would render a U.S. agency ineffectual.

The 9/11 Commission's rejection of the idea of a U.S. counterpart to MI5 was tentative. It said a domestic intelligence agency wasn't needed *if* the commission's other recommendations were adopted.[6] Many of them were whittled down by the Intelligence Reform Act and Terrorism Prevention Act of 2004, the legislative response to the 9/11 Commission's report. Recommendations for reorganizing congressional oversight of intelligence, to which the commission attached great importance, were ignored. So we don't know what the commission would think of the idea today—or at least we didn't know until the commission decided to reconstitute itself (albeit as a private, no longer a governmental, commission, the 9/11 Discourse Project).[7] The commissioners have been so taken aback by the FBI's inability to rectify the errors identified in the commission's report of July 2004 that they are now wondering whether the creation of a separate domestic intelligence agency mightn't be the right course of action after all.[8]

5. Scot J. Paltrow, "Secrets and Spies: U.K. Agency Makes Gains in Terror War; Can It Work Here?" *Wall Street Journal*, Oct. 6, 2004, p. A1.

6. *Final Report*, note 3 above, at 423.

7. Philip Shenon, "Sept. 11 Panelists Seeking U.S. Data on Terror Risks," *New York Times* (final ed.), June 6, 2005, p. A1.

8. "The FBI has stumbled badly in its attempts to remake itself since the Sept. 11, 2001, attacks and is plagued by high turnover, poor training and its continued inability to build a modern computer system, according to a panel

Amid mounting criticisms, which I summarize below, of the FBI's continuing inability to perform the domestic intelligence role adequately, the President in June of this year ordered the Bureau to build a halfway house to a true domestic intelligence agency by combining its three divisions that have intelligence responsibilities into a new unit to be called the "National Security Service" (NSS).[9] Because two of these divisions have law enforcement as well as intelligence duties (nor is it even clear that the intelligence activities of the new entity will be limited to national security intelligence), it will not be a true domestic intelligence agency, quite apart from its being lodged in a police department.

The United States *may* be right to refuse to create a domestic intelligence agency separate from the police and other countries wrong (or right for them but not for us). We are larger and more diverse, have a more robust civil liberties tradition, and face a wider range of threats. But the fact that we are out of step should give us pause. Although we are different from other countries, they are also different from each other (India versus France or Canada, for example), yet they agree on the need to separate domestic intelligence from law enforcement. It is no surprise,

convened yesterday by the members of the commission that investigated the terror strikes. The problems are so acute that members of the influential commission may want to reconsider whether the United States needs a separate agency to handle domestic intelligence, one Democratic member said." Dan Eggen, "FBI Fails to Transform Itself, Panel Says: Former Sept. 11 Commission 'Taken Aback' by Personnel, Technology Problems," *Washington Post*, June 7, 2005, p. A4.

9. George W. Bush, Memorandum, "Strengthening the Ability of the Department of Justice to Meet Challenges to the Security of the Nation," White House, June 29, 2005, www.fas.org/irp/news/2005/06/wh062905-doj.html; Douglas Jehl, "Bush to Create New Unit in F.B.I. for Intelligence," *New York Times* (national ed.), June 30, 2005, p. A1; David Johnston, "Antiterror Head Will Help Choose an F.B.I. Official: A Focus on Intelligence: Under Pressure, Bureau Will Cede a Piece of Its Prized Autonomy," *New York Times* (final national ed.), June 12, 2005, § 1, p. 1.

therefore, that criticisms of their approach that are based on the supposedly unique characteristics of the United States turn out to be superficial. One such criticism is that "if the Homeland Security Department and 170,000 people to be integrated is going to take a couple of years, standing up a brand new domestic intelligence agency would take a decade."[10] Another is that "We're not England. We're not 500 miles across our territory. We have thousands of miles to cover. Would you propose to create an organization that had people all over the United States, as the FBI does?"[11] The first criticism overlooks the fact that creating a domestic intelligence agency cannot be compared with the creation of the Department of Homeland Security, a mega-agency that dwarfs the entire domestic intelligence community. We'll see later that the total number of federal employees exclusively engaged in domestic intelligence probably does not exceed 7,000, which is fewer than 4 percent of the number of employees of DHS. In addition, it is more difficult to consolidate a number of heterogeneous agencies into a single department than to create a new agency that, as outlined in chapter 3 of this monograph, might have as a few as 1,500 employees.

As for the second criticism, although we are indeed not England a domestic intelligence agency would not require much field staff because its creation would not entail removing staff from the FBI. The Bureau would continue to play a large role in domestic intelligence.

10. Excerpts of testimony from Louis J. Freeh and Janet Reno in *The 9/11 Investigations: Staff Reports of the 9/11 Commission, Excerpts from the House-Senate Joint Inquiry Report on 9/11, Testimony from Fourteen Key Witnesses, including Richard Clarke, George Tenet, and Condoleezza Rice* 257, 264 (Steven Strasser, ed., 2004). The correct number of employees for the Department of Homeland Security is 180,000.

11. Remarks of William Webster quoted in Senate Select Commitee on Intelligence and House Permanent Select Committee on Intelligence, *Joint Inquiry into Intelligence Community Activities before and after the Terrorist Attacks of September 11, 2001* 351 (Dec. 2002).

The critics are correct that other nations tend to be more centralized than the United States. The United Kingdom, for example, has only 56 police forces; the United States has more than 20,000. Domestic intelligence has to liaise with local law enforcement, whose personnel may turn up clues to the existence of terrorist or prototerrorist gangs and to the identity of members, sympathizers, and foreign contacts. Also, terrorists sometimes commit quite ordinary crimes to finance their terrorist activities—bank robberies are a traditional example—though this has not been characteristic of recent terrorist activity in this country.

It is easier for thousands of local police departments, many quite small, to communicate with one federal agency than with two. But, at most, all that this would require is that in the division of responsibilities among agencies conducting domestic intelligence, responsibility for liaison with local police forces remain with the FBI. (Even before September 11, 2001, the FBI had established Joint Terrorism Task Forces with local law enforcement authorities; these task forces now exist in scores of cities.) But the qualification "at most" deserves emphasis. Because the FBI's relations with local authorities in regard to national security intelligence are strained,[12] leaving the liaison responsibility entirely to the FBI would be a mistake.

The FBI's Failures

The FBI is not the answer to the problem of domestic intelligence. As demonstrated by the 9/11 Commission's report, the Bureau turned in the most lackluster performance of any agency

12. The FBI isn't loved by local law enforcers, and a new intelligence agency would be free from the traditions and rivalries that inhibit day-to-day cooperation now. A "hat in hand" (with money) and "I'm not competing with you, I need you") attitude of the new agency would make local law enforcement more likely to cooperate in providing information and in making available suspects to be "turned" rather than arrested and prosecuted. For further discussion, see chapter 3.

in the run-up to 9/11,[13] even though it had (and has) the primary responsibility among police and intelligence services for preventing terrorist attacks on the nation from within. A request by one of the FBI field offices to apply for a warrant to search the laptop of Zacarias Moussaoui (a prospective hijack pilot) was turned down. A prescient report on flight training by Muslims in Arizona was ignored by FBI headquarters. There were only two analysts on the Bin Laden beat in the entire Bureau. Director Louis Freeh's directive that the Bureau focus its efforts on counterterrorism was ignored.

Concerning the Moussaoui episode, Senator Richard Shelby, the vice chairman of the Senate Select Committee on Intelligence, has pointed out that "FBI Headquarters actually *prohibited* intelligence investigators in Minneapolis from notifying the Criminal Division at the Justice Department about the Moussaoui situation, and *prohibited* agents from pursuing a criminal search warrant against him."[14] "The Bureau did not know what information it possessed, it did not approach this information with an intelligence analysis mindset, and it too often neglected to inform

13. For other criticism of the FBI's pre-9/11 performance as an antiterrorist agency, see U.S. Dept. of Justice, Office of the Inspector General, *A Review of the FBI's Handling of Intelligence Information Related to the September 11 Attacks* (Nov. 2004), www.justice.gov/oig/special/0506/final.pdf, summarized in Eric Lichtblau, "Report Details F.B.I.'s Failure on 2 Hijackers: Follow-Up Is Faulted on 9/11 Intelligence," *New York Times*, June 10, 2005, p. A1; Anonymous (Michael Scheuer), *Imperial Hubris: Why the West Is Losing the War on Terror* 185–191 (2004); *Joint Inquiry*, note 11 above, at 6, 243–246, 357–359 (Dec. 2002); Staff Statement No. 9, "Law Enforcement, Counterterrorism and Intelligence Collection in the United States prior to 9/11," in *The 9/11 Investigations*, note 10 above, at 239–256; Odom, *Fixing Intelligence*, note 5 above, ch. 8; and the Shelby statement, cited in the next footnote.

14. "September 11 and the Imperative of Reform in the U.S. Intelligence Community: Additional Views of Senator Richard C. Shelby, Vice Chairman, Senate Select Committee on Intelligence," Dec. 10, 2002, pp. 52–53, www.fas .org/irp/congress/2002_rpt/shelby.pdf. All emphases in my quotations from Shelby's statement are his.

other agencies of what it *did* know or believe."[15] Senator Shelby concluded that,

> though still renowned for its criminal investigative competence, the FBI has shown a disturbing pattern of collapse and dysfunction in its counterintelligence and counterterrorism functions. These recurring problems have, in turn, led many observers— and Members of Congress—increasingly to lose faith in the Bureau's ability to meet the national security challenges it faces, despite a series of internal reorganizations over the past several years that have failed to rectify the situation.
>
> In light of the FBI's dismal recent history of disorganization and institutional incompetence in its national security work, many of us in Congress have begun to consider whether it might better serve the interests of the American people to separate the counterintelligence and counterterrorism function of the Bureau into an entirely separate organization—one that would be free of the structural, organizational, and cultural constraints that have greatly handicapped the FBI's ability to conduct the domestic intelligence work our country depends upon it to perform.[16]

The reasons the Senator gave for the FBI's dysfunction as an intelligence agency are illuminating:

> Fundamentally, the FBI is a law enforcement organization: its agents are trained and acculturated, rewarded and promoted within an institutional culture the primary purpose of which is the prosecution of criminals. Within the Bureau, information is stored, retrieved, and simply *understood* principally through the conceptual prism of a "case"—a discrete bundle of information the fundamental purpose of which is to prove elements of crimes against specific potential defendants in a court of law.
>
> The FBI's reification of "the case" pervades the entire organization, and is reflected at every level and in every area: in the autonomous, decentralized authority and traditions of the Field Offices; in the priorities and preference given in individual career

15. Id. at 67.
16. Id. at 61–62.

paths, in resource allocation, and within the Bureau's status hierarchy to criminal investigative work and *post hoc* investigations as opposed to long-term analysis; in the lack of understanding of and concern with modern information management technologies and processes; and in deeply-entrenched individual mindsets that prize the production of evidence-supported narratives of defendant wrongdoing over the drawing of probabilistic inferences based upon incomplete and fragmentary information in order to support decision-making. . . . Far from embracing probabilistic inference, "knowledge" in a law enforcement context aspires—in its ideal form at least—not only to *certainty* but also to *admissibility*, the two essential conceptual elements of being able to prove someone guilty beyond a reasonable doubt in a court of law. Within such a paradigm, information exists to be *segregated* and ultimately employed under carefully-managed circumstances for the single specific purpose for which it was gathered.[17]

After 9/11 the Bureau, under a new director, Robert Mueller, vowed to do better, but his efforts[18] have fallen far short of success.[19] In part because the Bureau has been plagued by excessive turnover in the executive ranks of its intelligence and antiterrorism sections,[20] and even more so in its information technology staff, it took the Bureau two years after 9/11 just to devise a *plan*

17. Id. at 62–63.

18. Summarized in U.S. Department of Justice, Federal Bureau of Investigation, *Report to the National Commission on Terrorist Attacks upon the United States: The FBI's Counterterrorism Program since September 2001* (Apr. 14, 2004).

19. Staff Statement No. 12, "Reforming Law Enforcement, Counterterrorism, and Intelligence Collection in the United States" (National Commission on Terrorist Attacks Upon the United States, Staff Report, Apr. 14, 2004); Testimony of Dick Thornburgh, Chairman, Academy Panel on FBI Reorganization (National Academy of Public Administration, June 18, 2003).

20. Dan Eggen, "FBI Names 6th Antiterrorism Chief since 9/11," *Washington Post*, Dec. 29, 2004, p. A17. "All of the FBI's senior positions have turned over at least once since the Sept. 11 attacks, and many have changed hands numerous times." Id.

to reform its counterterrorism program.[21] We know now that the plan was a failure; for otherwise the President would not be forcing a reorganization on the Bureau.

Three and a half years after acknowledging in the wake of 9/11 the inadequacy of its information technology for intelligence purposes, the Bureau abandoned a $170 million "Virtual Case File" project intended to enable FBI agents to input intelligence data into their computers without having to undergo "a cumbersome, time-consuming process of preparing a paper record of that information, seeking the necessary approvals, then uploading the document into an existing database."[22] Because the FBI chose to develop Virtual Case File noncollaboratively, the federal and many of the state agencies with which it works delayed upgrading their own systems in the hope that by waiting until VCF was up and running they could configure their own systems to be compatible with the Bureau's.

The Bureau plans to take another three and a half to four years to complete the acquisition, at even greater (probably much greater) expense than that of the failed Virtual Case File system, of information technology adequate to the Bureau's needs.[23]

21. Laurie E. Ekstrand, "FBI Transformation: FBI Continues to Make Progress in Its Efforts to Transform and Address Priorities" 6 (U.S. General Accounting Office GAO-04-578T, Mar. 23, 2004).

22. Statement of Robert S. Mueller III, Director, Federal Bureau of Investigation, before the U.S. Senate Committee on Appropriations, Subcomittee, on Commerce, Justice, State and the Judiciary, Feb. 3, 2005, www.fbi.gov/congress/congress05/mueller020305.htm. The Virtual Case File fiasco is vividly described in Dan Eggen, "FBI Pushed Ahead with Troubled Software," *Washington Post*, June 6, 2005, p. A1.

23. Griff Witte, "FBI Outlines Plans for Computer System: Program Will Replace Canceled Project," *Washington Post*, June 9, 2005, p. A19; Eric Lichtblau, "F.B.I. Ends a Faltering Effort to Overhaul Computer Software," *New York Times* (late ed.), Mar. 9, 2005, p. A16; Larry Greenemeier, "Tech vs. Terrorism: The FBI Stumbled Badly in Modernizing Its IT to Help Fight Terrorism. Here's How the Bureau Plans to Get on Track," *InformationWeek*, June 6, 2005, www.informationweek.com/story/showArticle.jhtml?articleID=164300083. The most

What Senator Shelby said about the Bureau's unhappy experience with information technology in December 2002 remains true today: "In addition to these cultural and organizational problems—or perhaps in large part because of them—the FBI has never taken information technology (IT) very seriously, and has found itself left with an entirely obsolete IT infrastructure that is wholly inadequate to the FBI's current operational needs, much less to the task of supporting sophisticated all-source intelligence fusion and analysis."[24] As recently as June 2005, more than three and a half years after the 9/11 attacks, FBI officials were acknowledging "that they must radically change the agency's culture if the Bureau is ever going to get the high-tech analysis and surveillance tools it needs to effectively fight terrorism. The FBI, they say, must move from a decentralized amalgam of 56 field offices that are deeply distrustful of technology, outsiders and each other."[25]

One reason for the delays in, and inordinate expense of, the FBI's program for upgrading its information technology is that, consistent with the Bureau's emphasis on criminal investigation—its traditional core function—the program is not limited to intelligence. It encompasses the entirety of the FBI's operations, and the resulting scope and ambition of the program endanger its success because criminal investigation and national security intelligence have different methods and priorities, and the com-

complete account of the FBI's information technology troubles that I have read is Allan Holmes, "Change Management: Why the G-Men Aren't I.T. Men," *CIO Magazine*, June 15, 2005, www.cio.com/archive/061505/gmen.html.

24. "September 11 and the Imperative of Reform," note 14 above, at 72. For a recent example, see Wilson P. Dizard III, "Justice IG, FBI Spar over IT Management of Terrorist Watch List," *GCN* (*Government Computer News*), June 20, 2005, www.gcn.com/24_15/news/36133-1.html, reporting that the inspector general of the Justice Department has found that the Terrorist Screening Center, which is operated by the FBI, "has suffered from poor IT management and that its database is riddled with errors."

25. Holmes, note 23 above.

promises needed to satisfy both sets of users are difficult to devise and carry out. Because investigations of ordinary crimes can yield information of value to national security intelligence collectors, there is value in having a single database for everything in the FBI's files. But that value has to be traded off against the cost, delay, and possible failure of so ambitious a venture.

Not that even the ambitious venture *should* fail; for it is not *that* ambitious, given the vast storage capacity and search capability of today's commercial off-the-shelf computer software. Google enables near-instantaneous searching of eight billion web pages; Amazon.com enables near-instantaneous matching of millions of people with millions of products. The adaptation of these mature technologies to the needs of the FBI for data storage, retrieval, sorting, and matching should be straightforward. Ten thousand FBI special agents doing four reports a day of 250 words each (about 4 pages) 250 days a year for 10 years would produce a total of 100 million pages. That sounds like a lot but is only one-eightieth of the amount of data that can be searched by means of the Google search engine.[26]

The Failures Are Rooted in Structure

I am generally skeptical of organizational solutions to intelligence problems, most of which are not organizational problems.[27] But the FBI's inadequate performance of the domestic intelligence function is a genuine and serious organizational problem. Placing the domestic intelligence function in a criminal investigation agency ensures, as other nations realize, a poor fit. "'Mixing law

26. For examples of the type of commercial software that seem readily adaptable to intelligence needs, see John Markoff, "By and for the Masses," *New York Times* (final ed.), June 29, 2005, p. C1.

27. That skepticism is a major theme of my book *Preventing Surprise Attacks: Intelligence Reform in the Wake of 9/11* (2005).

enforcement with counterintelligence' simply cannot work. . . . 'Cops' cannot do the work of 'spies.'"[28]

Criminal investigation is retrospective. A crime has been committed and the investigators go about trying to find the criminal, and when they do they arrest him[29] and continue gathering evidence that will be admissible in court to prove his guilt. If the criminal activity under investigation is by nature ongoing, as in the case of gang activity, the investigator may decide to allow it to continue until the activity generates irrefutable evidence of guilt. But then he will pounce. And at every stage he'll take great care not to commit a procedural violation that might jeopardize a conviction. He will also balk at sharing with others any of the information that he obtains in his investigation, lest a leak tip off a suspect or make it easier for the suspect to defend himself in court should he be prosecuted. All that the sharing of information about a case can do from the FBI agent's perspective (as well as that of the local U.S. Attorney, whose support the agent requires) is to weaken his ability to control the future of the case.

Criminal investigation is case oriented, backward looking, information hugging, and fastidious (for fear of wrecking a prosecution). Intelligence, in contrast, is forward looking, threat oriented rather than case oriented, free wheeling. Its focus is on identifying, and maintaining surveillance of, suspicious characters and on patiently assembling masses of seemingly unrelated data into patterns that are suggestive of an emergent threat but that may be based on speculative hypotheses far removed from

28. "September 11 and the Imperative of Reform," note 14 above, at 74. For other reservations about the use of the criminal law to deal with terrorism, see Keith Johnson and David Crawford, "Do Jails Breed Terrorists? In Europe, Threat Seems to Be Exacerbated, Not Blunted, in Prison," *Wall Street Journal*, June 20, 2005, p. A13.

29. Sometimes the arrest is made by local police officers and the matter is then referred to the Justice Department for prosecution with the aid of the FBI; I shall disregard that detail, which is irrelevant to my analysis.

probable cause, let alone from proof beyond a reasonable doubt. When intelligence is working well, the spy or traitor or terrorist is detected early, before he does damage, and often he can be turned to our advantage. The orientation of intelligence toward preventing crimes from occurring or even from being contemplated, rather than toward prosecution after they occur, would prevent a domestic intelligence agency from obsessing over procedural missteps that might jeopardize a conviction.

The FBI argues that because terrorist acts are criminal and intelligence is an element of criminal law enforcement—notably in the case of "victimless crimes," where (by definition) law enforcement authorities cannot sit back and wait for a victim to complain but must penetrate the criminal gang much as in an intelligence operation directed against a terrorist group—counterterrorism intelligence can be assimilated to the FBI's criminal law enforcement responsibilities. However, the activities with which national security intelligence is concerned differ greatly from ordinary federal crimes. Terrorist activities are politically motivated (in a broad sense of "political" that includes motivations founded on religious, class, racial, or ethnic hostility) and are potentially much more dangerous than nonpolitical crimes because they aim to injure or destroy the nation as a whole, or entire population groups, or vital institutions, or otherwise wreak havoc on a large scale. To counter terrorist activity requires knowledge—of political movements, foreign countries and languages, the operational methods of terrorists, spies, and saboteurs, and the characteristics and availability of weapons of mass destruction—that criminal investigators do not possess. It also requires a different mind-set. Good police officers learn to think like criminals; good intelligence officers learn to think like terrorists and spies. The hunter must be empathetic with (as distinct from sympathetic to) his quarry. Cops and spies have different quarry.

As explained by intelligence veteran William Odom,

FBI officials want arrests and convictions. They want media attention and lots of it. FBI operatives want to make arrests, to "put the cuffs on" wrongdoers. They have little patience for sustained surveillance of a suspect to gain more intelligence. They prefer to gamble on an early arrest and an intimidating interrogation that might gain a confession. To them, sharing intelligence is anathema. Intelligence is something to be used, not shared. . . . Intelligence officials do not want public attention. They want to remain anonymous. They do not need arrest authority. They want to follow spies and terrorists secretly, allowing them to reveal their co-conspirators. Their reward comes from providing intelligence to others, not hiding it. . . . [They] tend to be more thorough, taking their time to develop evidence both for trials and for operational use. They know that they cannot let spies or terrorists get away without risking considerable danger to the country. Cops worry much less that a criminal will get away. Criminals are abundant and there are plenty more to arrest. Spies and terrorists will almost always defeat police officers. Spies and terrorists are normally backed by large state bureaucracies or non-state organizations with abundant resources and worldwide operational support. Criminals seldom are. Thus FBI techniques of recruiting "stoolies," tapping phones and conducting rough interrogations often work with mobsters but not with spies and terrorists.[30]

"Cops worry much less that a criminal will get away. . . ."

30. Odom, "Why the FBI Can't Be Reformed," note 4 above. In a reply to Odom, the FBI's deputy director made two points. The first is that terrorists may engage in ordinary crimes in order to finance their terrorist activities. The second is that the FBI "is capable of transforming itself in response to changing threats," and here he notes the impending creation of the National Security Service within the Bureau. John S. Pistole, "An FBI That Changes with the Times," *Washington Post*, July 8, 2005, p. A22. But he does not say that the terrorist groups with which we are most concerned today are likely to commit ordinary crimes inside the United States; nor does he explain why, if the FBI is capable of transforming itself, it has failed to do so and indeed strongly resisted the proposal to create the NSS.

Criminal law enforcement is oriented toward punishment, but punishment cannot undo the consequences of a catastrophic attack.[31] Criminal law aims to deter crime by punishing a large enough fraction of offenders to make the threat of punishment credible, as well as to incapacitate those offenders whom the threat of punishment did not deter from committing crimes, by locking them up or in extreme cases by executing them. Especially because many of the most dangerous modern terrorists are largely undeterrable, notably suicide bombers, who because their first successful attack is their last cannot be incapacitated after that attack to prevent them from repeating it, law enforcement alone cannot defeat terrorism.[32]

It can actually impede the struggle against terrorism: sometimes by prematurely revealing what the government knows, thus giving the terrorists a chance to elude capture by changing their methods or locale; at other times by failing to intervene early

---

31. Philip B. Heymann, *Terrorism and America: A Commonsense Strategy for a Democratic Society* 129–130 (1998), points out that criminal law enforcers are likely to "have little interest in all but the first two of the following eight questions that are critical to prevention" of terrorism: "[1] Who are the members actively engaged in planning to use violence for political purposes? [2] What is their motivation? [3] Where are they located? [4] Who in the population is likely to join the group or provide forms of support needed for its continued operations? [5] What is the extent and nature of the support the group is receiving from others outside the country, including another state? [6] How does the group handle the problems of remaining clandestine and yet carrying out political violence? What is its *modus operandi*? [7] What type of attacks is the group capable of? [8] What is the strategy behind their planning?"

32. The qualification "largely" is important, however. Even suicide bombers are deterrable in the following sense: if they know they're highly likely to be intercepted before they can detonate their bombs, they may decide to switch to another activity, because the expected benefit of their suicidal attack will have been reduced. By "expected benefit" I mean the benefit (as the suicide bomber would perceive it) of a successful attack, discounted (multiplied) by the probability that the attack would be successful.

enough (that is, before a crime has been committed). Melissa Mahle points out that

> the preparation stage [of terrorist attacks is] . . . the most vulnerable to detection and disruption, and the execution [stage] . . . the most difficult to disrupt. The preparation stage, which includes recruiting, training, casing, and putting support assets in place, requires more people and more movement than the execution phase. . . . All of these activities [undertaken by al Qaeda in preparation for the 9/11 attacks] required the movement of people and money and communication between cells, creating a hum of activity that intelligence assets are trained to pick up. The FBI caught some pieces, but made no attempt to assemble them into a larger picture.[33]

Identifying, assessing, and tracking activities in the preparation stage are quintessential intelligence tasks, but the activities themselves often are too ambiguous to be readily provable as crimes. Some are only minor crimes, some not crimes at all. Prosecuting persons suspected of being involved in the early stages (discussion, target surveillance, etc.) of preparing a terrorist attack may, when feasible, have value in deterring entry into that stage. Yet often the more effective strategy is not to arrest and prosecute at that stage but rather to monitor the suspects in an effort to learn the scope, intentions, membership, and affiliations of the terrorist or prototerrorist cell. A terrorist plot, once detected, can be disrupted without a trip to court. ("Hi, we're the 6 o'clock news team, and we hear you're up to no good.") An agency that is not responsible for bringing criminals to justice can concentrate full time on pursuing terrorists without any of the distractions created by the complex demands of criminal justice (including concerns with discovery and proof). Success from the standpoint of intelligence can be chasing terrorists out of the

33. Melissa Boyle Mahle, *Denial and Deception: An Insider's View of the CIA from Iran-Contra to 9/11* 327–328 (2004).

country and making sure they don't return, or even leaving them in place but turning them into government informants.

But detecting threats and preempting them before they are carried out may leave no room for successful prosecution—which is a clue to the difficulty of adapting a law enforcement agency to the intelligence role. Prosecutable crime is the life blood of law enforcement. The goal of law enforcement is to prevent crime, but the means is to prosecute criminals.

A classic of domestic intelligence was MI5's "double-cross system" in World War II.[34] MI5 succeeded in obtaining control over all the German spies in England and in using them to feed false and misleading information back to Germany. Prosecuting all of them—the instinctive law enforcement response—would have prevented a triumph of disinformation. Similarly, the proper aim of counterterrorism is to penetrate and control terrorist cells, not to cause their members to scatter as soon as the arrest of one rings a warning bell to the others. Penetration, "turning," control, disinformation are delicate intelligence operations requiring specialized skills, training, and aptitudes unlikely to be acquired and honed by FBI special agents converted temporarily into intelligence operatives.

In 2002, the FBI arrested in Lackawanna, New York, six men of Yemeni descent who had attended an al Qaeda training camp in Afghanistan. Jeff Smith, a former CIA general counsel, "explained how a domestic intelligence service could have done the job differently. An intelligence agency might have infiltrated the group, 'flipped' one or more of its members into double agents, then used them to get closer to higher levels of al Qaeda. . . . Instead, the individuals accused of being part of al Qaeda were arrested and charged in Buffalo in a highly publicized case.

34. J. C. Masterman, *The Double-Cross System in the War of 1939 to 1945* (1972).

'There is enormous pressure to prosecute these guys. . . . I have reluctantly come to the view that it just doesn't work to have intelligence and law enforcement within the same agency.'"[35]

An exchange between Senator Jay Rockefeller and Richard Clarke during the joint congressional inquiry into the 9/11 intelligence failure flagged the difficulty of fitting national security intelligence into the FBI's organizational culture:

> MR. ROCKEFELLER: One more question, and that is in the FBI where you have people investigating crimes that have taken place traditionally, they don't put something on the Internet, because their Internet doesn't work. They can't communicate with each other even if they did that, but they don't because they prefer to have case files, and so would I. . . . I am trying to do something, and I carry around my information in a folder, and that is mine, and I have worked on that. And it is not just proprietary, it is good prosecution potential. Now, that is an enormous mind-set which fights against a lot of what you have been talking about. How does that get overcome?

> MR. CLARKE: Well, I think there are two problems there that have to be overcome: one, the notion of focusing on prosecution. When I would ask the FBI agents in the field, why aren't you going after these guys who are here violating their visas or committing petty felonies? You could get them thrown out of the United States because of that. You may not be able to prove in court they are a terrorist, but you could prove they are doing this or that minor infraction and get them thrown out. The answer was, the U.S. attorneys don't want us to bother with minor things like that. . . . The U.S. attorneys want and the head of the FBI office in our city wants big scalps on the wall, big prosecutions that result in long sentences. . . .
>
> The other thing we have to get over is the notion of with-

35. Martin Kady II, "Lawmakers Put Domestic Spy Agency on Their Agenda, *Congressional Quarterly Daily Monitor*, Oct 15, 2002.

> holding information from headquarters. . . . There was not an
> understanding of intelligence fusion within the FBI, that the
> way you really can put a case together across a country is by
> getting a little fact here and a little fact there and putting it
> all together.[36]

The law enforcer's approach to terrorism has the further disadvantages of causing intelligence data to be evaluated from the
too-limited perspective of its utility in building a criminal case,
and of retarding the sharing of information lest full credit for a
successful prosecution be denied the field office that began the
investigation. These disadvantages illustrate the difference,
which is fundamental, between collecting information for the
sake of knowledge and collecting it for the sake of building a
case. Criminal investigators want to collect enough information
to be able to prove their case (and having collected it, they want
to hoard it rather than share it) but not to provide ammunition
for the defendant's lawyer to use at trial. An impediment to the
FBI's embrace of information technology is the Bureau's traditional reluctance to retain complete records (including interview
notes and other working papers) of its investigations, lest defen-
dants use them to their advantage. Prosecutors have a legal duty
to turn over to defense counsel any exculpatory material in their
possession, and the Department of Justice has an "open files"
policy intended to induce guilty pleas by allowing a criminal
defendant's lawyer to read the Department's entire file on the
case.

A recent incident involving the arrests in New York of two
Muslim teenage girls whom the FBI suspected of wanting to

---

36. United States Senate Select Committee on Intelligence and U.S. House
of Representatives Permanent Select Committee on Intelligence, *Joint Inquiry
Briefing by Staff on U.S. Government Counterterrorism Organizations (before September 11, 2001) and on the Evolution of the Terrorist Threat and U.S. Response:
1986–2001* 61–62 (June 11, 2002).

become suicide bombers, and held in custody for six weeks, illus-
trates how emphasis on a criminal law response to terrorism can
impair vital "hearts and minds" strategies as well as (as may have
happened in the Lackawanna case) shut down inquiry prematurely. The arrest of the two girls caused indignation in the New
York Muslim community[37]—whose loyalty and goodwill (as the
FBI recognizes) are vital safeguards against domestic terrorism.
It is natural for a law enforcement agency to want to arrest a
person suspected of criminal activity. An intelligence agency,
rather than wanting the girls arrested, would want to discover
who had put the idea of becoming suicide bombers in their minds
(maybe no one). Its low-key investigation might culminate in simply a chat with the girls' parents. If the girls had a connection,
however indirect, with a terrorist cell, the publicity attendant
upon their arrest doubtless caused the members to scatter—and
to reconstitute the cell elsewhere, out of sight of the FBI.

Here is a further example of the "two cultures" problem. The
performance of criminal investigators, unlike that of intelligence
officers, can be evaluated by objective, indeed quantitative, criteria, such as number of arrests weighted by successful convictions, with successful convictions weighted in turn by length of
sentence imposed, amount of property recovered, and amount of
favorable publicity generated.[38] Intelligence officers cannot be
evaluated by such objective criteria; their successes are often
invisible, indeed unknowable. For example, the earlier a plot is
detected and disrupted, the more difficult it is to know whether
it ever had a chance of success. And information obtained by

37. Andrea Elliott, "You Can't Talk to an F.B.I. Agent That Way, or Can You?"
New York Times (final ed.), June 4, 2005, p. B1.

38. "The [FBI] rewarded agents based on statistics reflecting arrests, indict-
ments, and prosecutions. As a result, fields such as counterterrorism and counterintelligence, where investigations generally result in fewer prosecutions, were
viewed as backwaters." Staff Statement No. 9, note 13 above, at 239, 241.

intelligence officers may be only a small part of the total information that enabled a threat to be detected and thwarted.

This asymmetry of performance measurement makes it difficult for a police department to hire and retain able intelligence
officers. Able employees prefer objective to subjective performance criteria; they know they'll do better if they are judged by
such criteria than if their performance is evaluated by nonobjec-
tive, nonquantifiable, criteria that may include personality,
appearance, personal connections, and sheer luck.[39] Thus in an
agency such as the FBI that combines criminal investigation with
intelligence, the abler recruits will gravitate toward criminal
investigation. They may be required to undergo some intelligence
training and to do stints in intelligence jobs, but always they will
be looking to return to the main career track.

Henry Kissinger has remarked that "intelligence personnel in
the real world are subject to unusual psychological pressures.
Separated from their compatriots by security walls, operating in
a culture suspicious of even unavoidable secrecy, they are sur-
rounded by an atmosphere of cultural ambiguity. Their unadver-
tised and unadvertisable successes are taken for granted, while
they are blamed for policies that frequently result from strategic
rather than intelligence misjudgments."[40] This does not sound
like the description of an FBI agent, and it casts grave doubt on
the wisdom of the FBI's method of obtaining intelligence officers,
which is to provide intelligence training to its special agents, all
of whom are hired and trained as criminal investigators. "The
worlds of law enforcement and intelligence are far apart. They

39. Luis Garicano and Richard A. Posner, "Intelligence Failures: An Organi-
zational Economics Approach" (forthcoming in *Journal of Economic Perspectives*).
40. Henry Kissinger, "Better Intelligence Reform: Lessons from Four Major
Failures," in Senate Appropriations Committee, *Review of the 9/11 Commission's
Intelligence Recommendations: Hearings before the Committee on Appropriations,
United States Senate*, 108th Cong., 2d Sess., pp. 7, 9 (Sen. Hearing 108–614,
Sept. 21–22, 2004).

have different roles, different rules, and different cultures, and often they do not speak the same language."[41] The two "worlds" don't fit comfortably together in the same agency—let alone in the same individual, the special agent with intelligence training, who shuttles between the two worlds.

Most of the FBI's employees, including 90 percent of its special agents, as distinct from its support staff, are stationed in the Bureau's 56 field offices rather than in its Washington headquarters.[42] This geographic dispersal is another reflection of the Bureau's emphasis on criminal investigation and another impediment to the conduct of national security intelligence. Most federal crime is local and is prosecuted locally by one of the 96 U.S. Attorneys' offices, which like the FBI's field offices are scattered across the nation. The FBI agents in these offices essentially work for the U.S. Attorney, who is a prosecutor, not an intelligence official. The reluctance of the field offices to share information with each other (a factor in the Bureau's resistance to information technology) reflects both the local focus of the special agents and the objective criteria of advancement that I mentioned. No local office wants its cases "stolen," and its "numbers" thereby reduced, by another office to which it might have conveyed the results of its investigation of a crime. Hence the "office of origin" mentality that treats the field office that originates a case as its owner. But while most federal crime is local, the principal dangers to domestic security at present emanate from international terrorist groups. Clues to their activities may be scattered all over the world. Effective intelligence requires com-

41. Elizabeth Rindskopf, "Comment," in *U.S. Intelligence at the Crossroads: Agendas for Reform* 256 (Roy Godson, Ernest R. May, and Gary Schmitt, eds., 1995).

42. U.S. Dept. of Justice, Office of the Inspector General, *The Internal Effects of the Federal Bureau of Investigation's Reprioritization*, ch. 2 (Audit Report 04–39, Sept. 2004), www.usdoj.gov/oig/reports/FBI/a0439/final.pdf.

bining scraps of information regardless of geographic origin rather than allowing information to be sequestered in local offices.

I use "scraps" advisedly; it brings out still another problem with confiding domestic intelligence to the FBI. Because of the gravity of threats to national security, intelligence officers must track down any lead, however implausible, that might point to an attack that would endanger national security. Most of those leads lead nowhere, let alone to an arrest, prosecution, conviction, and sentence. Chasing such will-o'-the-wisps is alien to the police mentality, for in ordinary crime work police do not chase down every tip, lead, clue, etc. to possible criminal activity. The expected cost of the ordinary crime is, in most cases, too small to make such chases cost-justified. If a crime occurs, the FBI is not blamed; crimes are expected; 15,000 people are murdered in the United States every year. Terrorist attacks are not expected; because of their greater potential gravity, more effort must be expended on preventing them than police expend on preventing the commission of ordinary crimes. Hence the emphasis of national security intelligence on prevention, in contrast to the FBI's focus on apprehension.

The dominance of the Bureau's field offices reflects the passivity that characterizes criminal investigation. (This is related to emphasizing apprehension over prevention.) FBI agents are not beat officers, patrolling on foot or in squad cars. They are accustomed to waiting until they receive a complaint of possible criminal activity before swinging into action. They don't go looking for crimes in the offing. They resent and resist being told by headquarters to focus their resources in a particular area. Indeed, they resist prioritization, which might deprive them of ready targets of opportunity, such as a reference by a local police officer of a gun or narcotics case.

The marriage of criminal investigation and domestic intelligence in the FBI has complicated the coordination of domestic and foreign intelligence. Often the same suspects are tracked outside the United States by the CIA and inside by the FBI's intelligence divisions. Yet the CIA and FBI have a history of mutual suspicion and antipathy.[43] This had begun to diminish even before 9/11, especially at the top of the two agencies. But the cultural and procedural gulf between criminal investigations and intelligence operations remains, has been aggravated by recent efforts of the Bureau to snatch turf from the embattled CIA, and impairs coordination between the two agencies just as it does within the FBI.

An agency 100 percent dedicated to domestic intelligence would do better at it than the FBI, which is at most 20 percent intelligence[44] and thus at least 80 percent criminal investigation and in consequence is dominated by the criminal investigators. In the wake of 9/11, rather than create a separate national security intelligence service, the Bureau decided to give its special agents training in intelligence as well as in criminal investigation. This is a recipe for underspecialization, unfortunately now codified by the Intelligence Reform Act[45] and therefore probably unaffected by the new reorganization (discussed in chapter 2 of this monograph), making it all the more likely that the ablest recruits will pursue careers as criminal investigators rather than as intelligence officers.

Not all the intelligence *analysts* in the FBI are special agents, it is true; but their selection and utilization are further evidence of the mismatch between intelligence and crime fighting. Many

43. See, for example, Mark Riebling, *Wedge: The Secret War between the FBI and CIA* (1994).

44. See note 7, chapter 3. It is true that one-third of the FBI's budget is allocated to intelligence, but the FBI's financial controls and reporting do not distinguish clearly between national security and ordinary crimes intelligence or between law enforcement and intelligence responses to national security threats.

45. Intelligence Reform and Terrorism Prevention Act of 2004, §§ 2001(c)(2), (3).

have been recruited from the Bureau's clerical staff, have been given perfunctory training (lasting only five or seven weeks), and, not surprisingly in light of their origin and training, "are still asked to perform duties that are not analytical in nature, such as escort, trash and watch duty. . . . Escort duty is following visitors, such as contractors, around the F.B.I. office to ensure that they do not compromise security. Trash duty involves collecting all 'official trash' to be incinerated. Watch duty involves answering phones and radios."[46]

All this is unlikely to change despite the reorganization ordered by the President. The effective control of an organization requires some uniformity in compensation methods, recruitment, evaluation, promotion, and working conditions in order to minimize conflict, foster cooperation, and avoid confusion and uncertainty. If the missions assigned to the organization are too disparate—if their optimal performance requires different methods, personnel policies, supervisory structures, information technology, etc., if indeed, as in the case of criminal investigation and domestic intelligence, the missions are incompatible—the compromises necessary to impose the requisite minimum uniformity will cause performance of the missions to be suboptimal. If shoes came in only one size, they would be cheap to manufacture but most people would be poorly shod. Because criminal investigation is the dominant mission and prevailing culture of the Bureau, the inherent tensions between criminal investigation and national security intelligence continue, long after the shock of 9/11, to be resolved in favor of the former.

But if the FBI really "wants" to be a criminal investigation agency, how to explain its desire to dominate domestic intelli-

46. Eric Lichtblau, "F.B.I. Gets Mixed Review on Analysis," *New York Times* (national ed.), May 5, 2005, p. A22, quoting a report by the Justice Department's Office of Inspector General. There could be no better evidence of the low status of intelligence in the FBI.

gence? Why isn't it happy to cede that function to a new agency? Why is it adamant in resisting the creation of such an agency even if its own intelligence capabilities are preserved? There are several reasons. A government agency that surrenders turf, even turf it doesn't particularly want, signals weaknesses that may invite further raids by competing agencies, as the CIA is learning to its sorrow. And because counterterrorism is now a national priority, an agency has budgetary and public-relations incentives, as well as reasons of prestige, to be given as large a role as possible in counterterrorism, of which a major tool is domestic intelligence. But because intelligence is an unpopular activity that stirs civil liberties concerns at both the Left and Right ends of the political spectrum and that yields fewer demonstrable successes than criminal prosecution, it is in the Bureau's interest to continue to place greater emphasis on the arrest and prosecution both of terrorist suspects and of ordinary criminals than on intelligence operations.

The FBI cannot be mollified by assurances that it will not be cut out of the intelligence business. A domestic intelligence agency would be competing with the Bureau for funds. Moreover, the Bureau may lack confidence that its intelligence model (combining national security intelligence with criminal investigation) is actually the superior one.

The WMD Commission's Critique

The objections to combining intelligence and criminal investigations in the same agency are not merely theoretical and comparative (other nations do it differently). They are also empirical. I gave examples earlier. Here I focus on the scathing critique of the FBI by the Commission on the Intelligence Capabilities of the United States Regarding Weapons of Mass Destruction ("WMD Commission" for short) led by former Senator Charles

Robb and Judge Laurence Silberman. The report, which devotes almost an entire chapter to the FBI's post-9/11 performance,[47] is even more critical of the Bureau than the 9/11 Commission's report had been. The reason may be that by the end of March 2005, when the WMD Commission issued its report, the FBI had had a full three and a half years since the 9/11 attacks to get its act together and, despite Mueller's efforts,[48] had failed to do so. Yet failure had been evident earlier. To quote Senator Shelby again,

> Despite repeated reorganizations, the FBI has simply performed too poorly for the American people to have much faith in its ability to meet current and future challenges no matter *how* many aggressive "reform" plans are announced by FBI management. Even a year after September 11, in fact, the FBI's deputy director sent angry e-mail messages to Bureau field offices declaring that he was 'amazed and astounded' that the Special

47. *Report of the Commission on the Intelligence Capabilities of the United States Regarding Weapons of Mass Destruction*, ch. 10 (Mar. 31, 2005).

48. Showcased in the Department of Justice report cited in note 18 above. This document, unsurprisingly, paints the FBI's efforts in the brightest possible hues. But it is unreliable. For example, it promised that the Virtual Case File system would be up and running within a year; within less than a year it was abandoned. Although the sunny report was submitted to Congress in April 2004, Mueller later testified that when the contractor "delivered the product [i.e., Virtual Case File] to us in December 2003, we immediately identified a number of deficiencies in VCF that made it unusable. Upon further examination [prior, however, to April 2004], we discovered nearly 400 problems with the software." Mueller, note 22 above. In like vein the FBI's parent, the Department of Justice, has been detected exaggerating the number of terrorist cases that it brings. U.S. General Accounting Office, "Report to the Honorable Dan Burton, House of Representatives: Justice Department: Better Management Oversight and Internal Controls Needed to Ensure Accuracy of Terrorism-Related Statistics," GAO-03-266, Jan. 2003, www.gao.gov/new.items/d03266.pdf; Mark Fazlollah, "Reports of Terror Crimes Inflated," *Philadelphia Inquirer*, May 15, 2003, p. A1. (Notice that more than two years elapsed between these two reports, evidently without any improvement occurring over that interval.) See also Dan Eggen and Julie Tate, "U.S. Campaign Produces Few Convictions on Terrorism Charges: Statistics Often Count Lesser Crimes," *Washington Post*, June 12, 2005, p. A1.

Agents in Charge (SACS) [of the field offices] *still* refused to commit essential resources to the fight against terrorism and *still* refused to share information properly with Headquarters.[49]

The WMD Commission remarked politely that the FBI had made "significant" (not substantial) progress since 9/11. But it gave no examples, while noting the Bureau's continued inability to acquire an adequate computer system and its chaotic organization, in which domestic intelligence is split up among three separate sections (intelligence, counterterrorism, and counterintelligence) and no one is in charge.

The commission reported that the FBI hopes to get its intelligence act together—by 2010 *at the earliest*.[50] The FBI's attitude, reflecting the domination of the Bureau by its scattered field offices, is typified by the remark of one of its officials that "Bin Laden is never going to Des Moines."[51] So if Bin Laden is smart he'll attack Des Moines because we now know it's unprotected. A successful attack on the heartland would be even more damaging to the morale of the American population as a whole than another attack on New York or Washington; no American would feel safe any longer.

The commission discovered that the Bureau had placed 96 percent of its intelligence budget in divisions not subject to the direct authority of the Director of National Intelligence and had given its Executive Assistant Director for Intelligence (a position not even filled until 18 months after the 9/11 attacks awoke the Bureau from its intelligence slumbers), who *is* subject to that authority, no power and virtually no staff. Another game FBI officials play is eliminating job descriptions that would place the

49. "September 11 and the Imperative of Reform," note 14 above, at 74–75.
50. "Even FBI officials acknowledge that its collection and analysis capabilities will be a work in progress until at least 2010." *Report of the [WMD] Commission*, note 47 above, at 29. That "at least" is at once astonishing and ominous.
51. Id. at 453.

jobholder under the authority of the Director of National Intelligence. These evasions may now end, with the new reorganization, but they remain illustrative of the FBI mind-set, which is unlikely to change.

The commission noted the FBI's "continued failure"—this after three and a half years of ostensible striving—"to institute the reforms necessary to transform the FBI into the intelligence organization it must become. . . . The FBI has not constructed its intelligence program in a way that will promote integrated intelligence efforts, and its ambitions have led it into unnecessary new turf battles with the CIA."[52] "While the FBI has made steps in the right direction since September 11, it has many miles to travel."[53] (It takes many steps to add up to even one mile.) "Can the FBI's latest effort to build an intelligence capability overcome the resistance that has scuppered past reforms? In our view, the effort this time is more determined, but *the outcome is still in doubt.*"[54]

Before the Intelligence Reform Act changed things, the FBI's Office of Intelligence was responsible mainly for training and

---

52. Id. at 451, 468.

53. Id. at 468. "Reform will require enormous commitment and effort within the FBI, as well as sustained outside coordination and oversight." Id. True; but there is insufficient commitment within the FBI, and, as a result, there will be insufficient effort.

54. Id. at 454 (emphasis added). The WMD Commission further criticized the FBI's efforts to "reinvent" itself as an intelligence agency in a March 29, 2005, letter to President Bush, www.wmd.gov/report/fbicia.pdf. The letter remarks, for example, that "the FBI proposes to 'integrate' law enforcement and national security in a way that makes it impossible to establish an integrated national security workforce, which you [i.e., President Bush] called for in November and which we believe is essential to the security of this country" (p. 2). "The FBI recognizes what is needed to integrate these three national security missions [intelligence, counterintelligence, and counterterrorism], *and rejects it*" (id.; emphasis added). The letter thus comes close to accusing the FBI of defying the President. For still other criticism of the FBI as an intelligence agency, see Gabriel Schoenfeld, "How Inept Is the FBI?" *Commentary*, May 2002, p. 53.

recruitment, but not for operations; they were the responsibility of the Bureau's Counterterrorism and Counterintelligence Divisions. The Act renamed the Office of Intelligence the Directorate of Intelligence and assigned it a variety of important tasks, including "supervision of all national intelligence programs, projects, and activities of the Bureau,"[55] but did not mention the other divisions. Six months after the Act was passed, the Directorate of Intelligence was *still* not in charge of the Bureau's national security intelligence; the heads of the other two divisions didn't report to the Directorate's chief. The Directorate remained an etiolated counterpart to the CIA's Directorate of Intelligence (the analytic branch), while the Counterterrorism and Counterintelligence Divisions corresponded to the CIA's Directorate of Operations.

So until the reorganization is completed, the FBI will not have a domestic intelligence service in any sense, but instead three services each having intelligence responsibilities—and criminal investigation responsibilities to boot. The Directorate of Intelligence is not limited to intelligence concerning terrorist or other threats to national security; it is also responsible for intelligence about ordinary criminal activities within the Bureau's jurisdiction. (Whether the reorganization will change this is unclear.) And the Counterterrorism and Counterintelligence Divisions are engaged in arresting and gathering evidence for prosecuting terrorists and spies, as well as in pure intelligence and counterintelligence. Indeed, the head of the Counterterrorism Division, rather than being an intelligence professional, began his career as a police officer and since becoming an FBI special agent in 1983 had, until 2004, been involved in criminal investigations rather than in intelligence.[56] FBI officials have

55. Intelligence Reform and Terrorism Prevention Act of 2004, Title II, § 2002(c)(1).

56. "About Us: FBI Executives," www.fbi.gov/libref/executives/hulon.htm.

acknowledged that the Bureau bases appointments to supervisory positions in intelligence on managerial experience rather than intelligence expertise.[57] This means that criminal investigators will continue to dominate intelligence because few of the Bureau's intelligence specialists have the requisite managerial experience.

57. John Solomon, "Terrorism Expertise Takes a Back Seat," *Inland Valley Daily Bulletin*, June 20, 2005, pp. A1, A5.

2. The "Agency within an Agency" Solution

The WMD Commission recommended that the FBI combine its three divisions that have intelligence responsibilities into a single entity. The FBI accepted the recommendation "under pressure from the White House . . . after a series of scathing reports that have criticized [the Bureau] for intelligence lapses."[1] "The plan represents a particularly sharp rebuke to the historically independent FBI, which has struggled to remake itself into a counterterrorism agency since the Sept. 11, 2001, attacks and has been the target of withering reviews from both inside and outside the government."[2]

The President's memorandum[3] announcing the reorganization gives few details; presumably much remains to be negotiated between the FBI and the Director of National Intelligence. But we know that the three divisions are to be consolidated into a "National Security Service" whose chief will have to be approved by the DNI but will report to the FBI director as well as to the DNI;[4] that its budget will be part of the National Intelligence

1. David Johnston, "Antiterror Head Will Help Choose an F.B.I. Official," *New York Times* (final national ed.), June 12, 2005, § 1, p. 1.

2. Dan Eggen and Walter Pincus, "Spy Chief Gets More Authority over FBI: Negroponte Will Control Bureau's Intelligence Side," *Washington Post*, June 30, 2005, p. A1.

3. See note 9, chapter 1.

4. According to Jay Solomon and Anne Marie Squeo, "Bush Team Takes Steps to Address U.S. Security Gaps," *Wall Street Journal*, June 30, 2005, pp. A3, A4, the head of the NSS will report to the deputy director of the FBI rather than to the director. The current deputy director, John Pistole (see note 30, chapter 1), like the head of the Bureau's Counterterrorism Division, is not a career

Program, which is to say the overall intelligence budget that the DNI submits to the President; and that the FBI is to establish procedures that will enable the DNI to communicate through the chief of the National Security Service with all FBI intelligence personnel in order to ensure that the Bureau's intelligence activities are coordinated with those of the other federal intelligence agencies.

Whether the reorganization will yield net benefits is uncertain. It seems a step in the right direction, but many pitfalls loom—fatal ones, in all likelihood, unless the reorganization is supplemented by the creation of a domestic intelligence agency separate from the FBI.[5] Every one of the following pitfalls points to the need for such an agency:

1. By subordinating the Bureau's intelligence function to the authority of the Director of National Intelligence, the President's order may precipitate the mother of all turf battles. The FBI is fiercely independent, popular with the general public, politically influential, and a past master of public relations; in contrast, the public is suspicious of intelligence ("spying"). Should the Bureau succeed in fending off the DNI's efforts to change its approach, all that the reorganization may amount to is somewhat better coordination between the Bureau's Directorate of Intelligence and its Counterterrorism and Counterintelligence Divisions—a modest success. And fierce turf battles will impose, at the least, high transition costs.

2. Even if the reorganization is spared debilitating turf wars, it will not be spared transition costs, because complex, time-consuming adjustments will be necessary to unite the three divisions into a single, effective, stand-alone unit. Remember that

---

intelligence officer. He had little or no intelligence experience before he became the deputy director of that division in 2002.

5. As I explain in chapter 3, the reorganization of the FBI can coexist with the proposals discussed in that chapter, including the creation of a true domestic intelligence agency.

the Directorate of Intelligence is responsible for ordinary-crimes intelligence as well as for national security intelligence and that the Counterterrorism and Counterintelligence Divisions have law enforcement as well as intelligence responsibilities. A simple fusion will not produce an intelligence agency, but a hybrid. It would be comparable to merging MI5 with the Special Branch of Scotland Yard. But extracting law enforcement activities directed against terrorists and spies from the Counterterrorism and Counterintelligence Divisions, so as to make the National Security Service a real intelligence agency rather than an MI5–Special Branch hybrid, is a daunting prospect.

Remember too that the intelligence analysts are poorly selected and deployed and that the intelligence officers are recycled special agents often hoping to cycle back to the criminal investigation career track. What is required is not merely a combining of the three units under a single leader but a complete shakeup of organization, personnel, training, and practices, lest the reorganization end up being nothing more than the interposition of a manager between the heads of the three units and the Bureau's director.

3. The plan of reorganization, at least as announced, says nothing about establishing a separate unit for information technology in the National Security Service. The service may be dependent on the Bureau's unpromising, overly ambitious, protracted follow-on to the failed Virtual Case File project.

4. The FBI has repeatedly reorganized its intelligence operation with little to show for its efforts. Furthermore, the history of government reorganizations teaches that most fail, *especially* those imposed on an agency from the outside.[6] The FBI announced reorganizations of its intelligence operation in 1998, 1999, 2001, and 2002. A further reorganization was decreed by

---

6. Richard A. Posner, *Preventing Surprise Attacks: Intelligence Reform in the Wake of 9/11* 158–159 (2005).

the Intelligence Reform Act in 2004, with no apparent effect.[7] Can still *another* reorganization be what the doctor ordered, especially one again imposed from the outside over strong resistance by the agency to be reorganized?

5. The head of the National Security Service will have too many bosses—the FBI's director and deputy director,[8] the Attorney General, and the DNI—complicating the command structure and undermining his authority. As the joint appointee of the FBI director and the DNI, he will know he has multiple masters whom he will have to try to satisfy despite their divergent interests and perspectives. Unlike the director of the CIA, he will not be a Presidential appointee. He will be the third-ranked subordinate of an official, the FBI director (the deputy director is the number two man in the Bureau), who, though a Presidential appointee, is himself subordinate to a department head, the Attorney General.

6. The FBI director may favor criminal investigation over intelligence even more than at present because he will be in full charge of criminal investigation but only half in charge of intelligence. He will be reluctant to designate any job position as "intelligence" because he will want to minimize oversight by the Office of the DNI.

7. When a vacancy occurs in the directorship of the FBI, there will be a cat fight over whether to fill it with an intelligence officer or with a criminal law enforcer.[9]

8. Often it is easier to create a new organization than to

7. For a comprehensive discussion of the FBI's efforts at intelligence reform, see Alfred Cumming and Todd Masse, *CRS Report for Congress: RL32336-FBI Intelligence Reform since September 11, 2001: Issues and Options for Congress* (Congressional Research Service, Apr. 6, 2004), www.au.af.mil/au/awc/awcgate/crs/rl32336.htm.

8. The head of the new service will report to the deputy director, not the director.

9. In time of war or acute national emergency, the former would seem clearly the better choice, with his principal deputy a criminal law enforcer.

reorganize an existing one. There is a long and on the whole successful history of starting new intelligence agencies, beginning with the Office of Strategic Services (OSS) in 1942. A reorganization threatens existing staff, and so is resisted and often in the process deformed, especially if agency staff has cultivated alliances with members and staff of Congress, as FBI officials have long done. Besides having to overcome passive and not so passive resistance by employees whose tenure or status the reorganization threatens, a reorganization disrupts work routines and scrambles lines of command, sowing confusion and disaffection that may take years to overcome.[10] Because creating a new agency would be easier than reorganizing the FBI, it would be an insurance policy against the possible failure of the reorganization.

9. Carving a domestic intelligence service out of an existing criminal investigation agency does nothing, at least in the short term, to change organizational culture. As Representative Jane Harman, the ranking Democrat on the House intelligence committee, has observed, successful reorganization of the FBI "will require a massive cultural change within the F.B.I., because the guns and badges and the mind-set of the F.B.I. don't totally fit with the challenges of countering terrorism."[11] The staff of the new entity will be the same staff that, imbued as it is with the Bureau's law enforcement culture, has conducted national security intelligence inadequately.

10. Creating a new organization offers the best opportunity for a genuinely fresh start that will enable us to learn whether the steady state that the established intelligence bureaucracies have attained is what the nation needs. A new agency will have no commitments; it can experiment with up-to-date ideas of "best

10. Posner, note 6 above, at 128–129; also reference in id. at 132 n. 11.
11. Douglas Jehl, "Bush to Create New Unit in F.B.I. for Intelligence," *New York Times*, June 30, 2005, p. A1. "Totally" understates the problem.

practices" whether or not they are accepted by the established agencies.

11. Unless the National Security Service is thoroughly encapsulated—impacted—within the FBI, it will be unable to disentangle itself from some of the worst features of the Bureau's present domestic intelligence operation, such as the computer imbroglio. Will the new agency have to wait three and a half to four years to obtain a computer system optimized for domestic intelligence, which as we know is the FBI's current schedule? If to be effective the National Security Service will have to be self-sufficient and cut most of its ties to the rest of the Bureau, what is the advantage of having it in the Bureau?

12. The reorganization may require legislation to implement. The Intelligence Reform Act creates the job title "Executive Assistant Director [of the FBI] for Intelligence"; places this official in charge of the Directorate of Intelligence; and assigns the Directorate responsibility for "supervision of all national intelligence programs, projects, and activities of the Bureau."[12] To place the directorate under a different official of the Bureau—the head of the National Security Service—will displace the statutory authority of the Executive Assistant Director for Intelligence. Nor, under the reorganization, will the Directorate of Intelligence occupy the role assigned it by the Act of supervising the intelligence operations of the Counterterrorism and Counterintelligence Divisions. It is possible, as I'll note in chapter 3, that Congress does not have the constitutional authority to micromanage the organization of national security agencies to the degree the Act attempts. But that is an open question at best, and uncertainty about the correct answer will cast a shadow over efforts to effectuate the reorganization purely by executive decree.

A particular concern is the provision of the Intelligence Re-

12. Intelligence Reform and Terrorism Prevention Act of 2004, Title II, §§ 2002(b), (c)(1).

form Act that requires FBI special agents to be trained as intelligence officers and to serve stints in both criminal investigation and intelligence rather than being allowed to specialize full time in intelligence. Unless repealed or ignored, this provision will prevent the National Security Service from achieving sufficient autonomy to be able to function effectively as an intelligence agency. Special agents will be shuttling back and forth between the NSS and the criminal investigation side of the Bureau.

13. The only way to discover whether the FBI is correct in thinking that national security intelligence should be centered in the Bureau is to create a competing entity that is not part of a criminal investigation agency and has no law enforcement powers. The FBI should welcome the opportunity to prove that its intelligence model is superior. But that is asking too much of human nature. No one likes having a competitor.

For all these reasons, it would be a mistake to count on the success of the reorganization to obviate the need for a separate domestic intelligence agency.

The following counterarguments have limited force:

1. The most seductive is that we should wait to see how the reorganization works; if we discover it has failed, we can lift the National Security Service out of the Bureau (cutting on the dotted line, as it were, drawn by the reorganization) and make it a separate agency. The possibility of that happening, coupled with strong pressure from the President, is a big motivation for the Bureau's taking the need for change seriously.

But the nation cannot afford the time that it would take to evaluate the results of a wait-and-see approach. The reorganization will take months or even years to implement fully, and during this period no one will be able to determine whether an effective domestic intelligence agency has been or is being created. If two years from now it is decided that the Bureau has had its chance and has blown it (the likeliest outcome), we will have lost two years in dealing with the terrorist menace.

Moreover, to lift the National Security Service out of the FBI would not be the correct response to the failure of the reorganization.[13] This is not only because the required surgery would be painful, but also because the service would take with it its police culture (the reason, no doubt, *why* the reorganization will have failed). The Canadian domestic intelligence agency was formed from the security service of the Royal Canadian Mounted Police. The service carried with it into its new home much of the culture of the RCMP, a police culture, which reduced the effectiveness of the new agency.

2. It might be thought that the FBI's prestige, and its continued popularity with the general public despite its intelligence failures, would make recruitment for the National Security Service easier than recruitment for a new domestic intelligence agency. But this is unlikely. People who want to be intelligence officers don't want to be part of a police force, and that is the perception that will prevail even if the National Security Service is placed in a watertight capsule. Moreover, being feared and disliked by major elements of a segment of the American public that is critical to domestic intelligence—namely the Arab American and (overlapping) Muslim American communities—the Bureau is having difficulty recruiting people with language skills essential to counterterrorist intelligence. Ever since the 9/11 attacks, the Bureau has treated those communities with a heavy hand,[14] as in the incident involving the arrest of the two teenage would-be suicide bombers. Animosity toward the Bureau has frustrated efforts even to hire translators and has left it with a

13. This represents a change of view for me. In chapter 6 of *Preventing Surprise Attacks*, note 6 above, I urged consideration of creating a domestic intelligence agency out of the intelligence-related units of the FBI. That now seems to me a mistake, for the reasons explained in the text.

14. See, for example, Juliette Kayyem, "Changing the Color of Intelligence," *Boston Globe* (third ed.), Aug. 3, 2004, p. A13.

mass of untranslated telephone intercepts that may contain undiscovered clues to (serious, adult) terrorist plans.[15]

It would be easier to recruit from these communities for an agency unconnected with the FBI. Since the aim would be to create a dominant intelligence culture in the new agency, its experienced officers would, with few exceptions, not come from the FBI. But there are plenty of other sources. Many able CIA officers with relevant skills who had retired before September 11, 2001, have been brought back to work in the intelligence community on contract, and some of them are ready for a new challenge. Others have left the CIA recently because they didn't like the beating the agency has been taking or could not manage careers overseas with spouses who have better-paying jobs in the United States; those ex-officers too are potential recruits. And recruiting and training new operations officers should not be as difficult or protracted as in the CIA, because operating within the United States is less demanding than adjusting to a foreign, often hostile environment.

3. Criminal investigations are a vital tool of national security.[16] In holding that warrants issued under the authority of the

15. Eric Lichtblau, "F.B.I. Said to Lag on Translations of Terror Tapes," *New York Times* (late ed.), Sept. 29, 2004, p. A1; Richard B. Schmitt, "Translation Capacity Still Spotty after 9/11," *Los Angeles Times* (home ed.), May 1, 2005, p. 24, summarizing U.S. Dept. of Justice, Office of the Inspector General, Audit Division, "The Federal Bureau of Investigation's Foreign Language Program—Translation of Counterterrorism and Counterintelligence Foreign Language Material" (Audit Report 04-25 July 2004), states that "three years after the Sept. 11 attacks, more than 120,000 hours of potentially valuable terrorism-related recordings have not yet been translated by linguists at the Federal Bureau of Investigation, and computer problems may have led the bureau to systematically erase some Qaeda recordings." See also Eric Lichtblau, "Inspector General Rebukes F.B.I. over Espionage Case and Firing of Whistle-Blower," *New York Times* (late ed.), Jan. 15, 2005, p. A8. The whistleblower, an FBI translator of Middle Eastern languages, had complained among other things about the Bureau's shoddy translation practices.

16. Jeff Breinholt, "Seeking Synchronicity: Thoughts on the Role of Domestic

Foreign Intelligence Surveillance Act for electronic or other surveillance may lawfully be used to gather evidence of criminal activity, the FISA review court said that

> arresting and prosecuting terrorist agents of, or spies for, a foreign power may well be the best technique to prevent them from successfully continuing their terrorist or espionage activity. The government might wish to surveil the agent for some period of time to discover other participants in a conspiracy or to uncover a foreign power's plans, but typically at some point the government would wish to apprehend the agent and it might be that only a prosecution would provide sufficient incentives for the agent to cooperate with the government. Indeed, the threat of prosecution might be sufficient to "turn the agent."[17]

The court added, however, that "punishment of the terrorist or espionage agent is really a secondary objective."[18] That is wormwood to the FBI.

Cooperation between intelligence officers and criminal investigators is unlikely to be greater within an agency torn between two mutually suspicious services than between two agencies with carefully demarcated jurisdictions (though there is nothing wrong with some overlap to provide redundancy and competition): an agency that has domestic intelligence responsibilities but no law enforcement responsibilities, and a law enforcement agency that conducts intelligence operations mainly in support of criminal investigations. Although the FBI is a part of the Justice Department, it takes an average of 46 days for the lawyers in the De-

---

Law Enforcement in Counterterrorism" (forthcoming in *American University International Law Review*).

17. In re *Sealed Case*, 310 F.3d 717, 724 (U.S. Foreign Intelligence Surveillance Court of Review 2002). Though cast in terms of state-sponsored terrorism or espionage, the court's analysis also has application to nonstate actors, such as al Qaeda, though perhaps with diminished force, as suggested by the statistics and references in Dan Eggen and Julie Tate, "U.S. Campaign Produces Few Convictions on Terrorism Charges," *Washington Post*, June 12, 2005, p. A1.

18. 310 F.3d at 744–745.

partment to present an application for a FISA warrant to the FISA court.[19] That is a sign of poor internal cooperation.

Scotland Yard's Special Branch specializes in the arrest and prosecution of terrorists; this may turn out to be the character of the FBI's new National Security Service. The NSS is unlikely to escape the gravitational pull of criminal investigation. Not only because of the Bureau's traditions and organizational culture— the stubborn culture to which Representative Harman and count- less others have attested—but also because ordinary crime fighting will always (one hopes) require greater resources than domestic intelligence. There is more crime than there is terror- ism, and it is costly to prepare a criminal prosecution.

And while a person wanting a career in intelligence will not be attracted to working in a police department, it is different with someone wanting a career in the criminal investigation of terrorists—a prestigious and exciting field of police work. Just as Scotland Yard's Special Branch cooperates with MI5,[20] so a pros- ecution-oriented NSS could be expected to cooperate with a U.S. domestic intelligence agency because it would no longer be in direct competition with it. The NSS would have a strong incen- tive to cooperate because the domestic intelligence agency would refer matters to it for prosecution.

There is another reason why such an agency would not step on the FBI's toes more than occasionally. The agency's remit would be limited to national security intelligence, which is to say intelligence concerning the gravest possible threats to the nation, rather than garden-variety criminal acts. The FBI, reflecting its law enforcement culture, classifies as "terrorism" virtually any

19. Eric Lichtblau, "Audit Finds Logjam in Efforts to Spy on Terror Suspects," *New York Times* (late ed.), Apr. 28, 2005, p. A20.

20. Not perfectly, of course, Center for Democracy and Technology, "Do- mestic Intelligence Agencies: The Mixed Record of the UK's MI5" 3 (Jan. 27, 2003); any interagency relationship is fraught.

politically motivated crime, a great deal of which, however, such as the attacks by the Animal Liberation Front on laboratories in which medical experiments are performed on animals, does not threaten national security. Minor terrorists are easier to catch and prosecute than major ones. And recall that the FBI, being reactive rather than proactive in its criminal investigatory work, is not accustomed to setting priorities.

The agency would be required to notify the Justice Department of serious criminal activity discovered in its investigations even if it opposed prosecution. The head of the agency would negotiate the disposition of the matter with the Attorney General.

4. The FBI works with the nation's police forces in investigating drug offenses, bank robberies, and other ordinary federal crimes; and local police forces, along with customs, visa, border-patrol, and other federal officers, should be the "ears and eyes" of a nationwide intelligence network. Yet the Bureau neither has nor should have a monopoly position in regard to such a network. Despite the formation of the Joint Terrorism Task Forces, the FBI has not succeeded in creating such a network, and many of the "ears and eyes" doubt that it has really tried. (More on this shortly.)

5. Criminal investigators have well-established criteria for determining what constitutes proof rather than mere grounds for suspicion, and familiarity with these criteria may prevent intelligence operatives from going off on wild goose chases. But this is just to say that a background in criminal investigation would be something a domestic intelligence service would want some of its employees to have. That is different from lodging the service in a criminal investigation agency.

Moreover, the rules of evidence that law enforcers are required to study and master are not just rules about separating proof from conjecture. Many of them are evidence-suppressing privileges, such as the privilege against self-incrimination, or are concerned with keeping from jurors evidence they're believed incapable of evaluating correctly. These blinders placed on the pursuit of truth in litigation don't belong in intelligence, which is not concerned with building a case and may be able to make fruitful use of conjectures, of hints far short of probable cause, of imaginative projections of unlikely horrors. A vivid imagination is not part of the normal equipment of police officers.

6. The FBI has investigative tools that a domestic intelligence agency would sometimes want to use as well, including access to the unit in the Justice Department that applies for warrants to conduct electronic surveillance under the Foreign Intelligence Surveillance Act and the power to obtain on demand access to phone bills (and other records of communications whether by wire or by electronic means), banking records, and credit reports.[21] With regard to applications for FISA warrants, however, statutory authority is lodged in the Attorney General rather than the Bureau,[22] and he could appoint the general counsel of a domestic intelligence agency as a special assistant to him to exercise his authority to apply for such warrants on behalf of the agency. Regarding banking and credit records, but not phone and other communications records, agencies other than the FBI can obtain these records if the agency is investigating "international terrorism,"[23] but investigations of purely homegrown terrorism are excluded.

So there is some power gap, and the FBI may be reluctant to cooperate with a competitor. This underscores the need for the Director of National Intelligence to assert control over domestic intelligence, as I discuss in chapter 3. If the FBI should not have a monopoly of domestic intelligence, neither should it

---

21. 18 U.S.C. § 2709; 12 U.S.C. § 3414(a)(5); 15 U.S.C. § 1681u.
22. 50 U.S.C. § 1804(a).
23. 12 U.S.C. § 3414(a)(1)(C); 15 U.S.C. § 1681v.

have a monopoly of the tools that a domestic intelligence agency would need for maximum effectiveness.

7. Domestic intelligence is a bugbear of civil libertarians, who argue that it is safer kept in the FBI because the Bureau is under the supervision of the Attorney General, the nation's chief legal officer. The argument is unsound—at its most basic level, because the Attorney General is a prosecutor rather than a judge, a defense lawyer, or a professional civil libertarian. To the Justice Department, civil liberties are a constraint, often an irksome one, not a mission. Civil libertarians did not like Attorney General John Ashcroft; they do not like his successor, Alberto Gonzales; and they continue to complain about what they consider to be the FBI's insensitivity regarding civil liberties.[24] There is more to be said on this sensitive issue, however, and I return to it in chapter 3.

8. Arguably, if given sufficient autonomy the National Security Service will be able to escape the surrounding police culture of the Bureau. But the argument points to a fundamental dilemma: If to change the culture the National Security Service is truly encapsulated, the potential benefits from combining intelligence and criminal investigation in one agency will evaporate. There would be no greater obstacles to cooperation between two formally separate agencies than there would be between two agencies that, though nominally joined, were separated by a Chinese wall. Yet without such separation, all that will have been accomplished by the reorganization is a tighter integration of the Bureau's intelligence, counterterrorism, and counterintelligence units, and that is a "solution" unresponsive to the concerns behind the reorganization. Intelligence will continue to be subordinated to and intermixed with criminal investigation, even

24. See, for example, Michael Dobbs, "FBI Monitored Web Sites for 2004 Protests," *Washington Post*, July 18, 2005, p. A3.

though that subordination and that intermixture are the underlying problems.

A recent editorial in the *Washington Post* expresses a common reaction to the reorganization. I quote the heart of the editorial writer's argument:

> Whether this transformation [of the FBI "into a credible intelligence organization"] is ultimately possible, however, remains an open question. The bureau has made more headway in developing intelligence capability than its fiercer critics acknowledge, but it remains, in its heart and soul, a police force. This culture may simply be too deeply rooted to be changed. At present, however, creating a domestic intelligence service is politically dicey; the step would have significant civil liberties implications and could create gaps in effectiveness that terrorists could exploit. Consequently, there is little choice but to proceed as the administration is proceeding—that is, reform the bureau with an ongoing eye to whether the project is, at the end of the day, a fool's errand. . . . The president's memorandum requires the government to "develop procedures" by which the director of national intelligence can "communicate with the FBI's field offices" through the new head of the National Security Service. Whether this presents a problem depends entirely on what these procedures turn out to be. It is essential that FBI agents collecting intelligence domestically are not directed by the White House or top administration officials but, rather, by the FBI director overseen by the attorney general. In implementing the president's order, the administration must remember that whatever agency is responsible for domestic intelligence must be kept independent of politics.[25]

The editorial expresses a sensible pessimism about the prospects for transformative change in the FBI. But it veers off the track when it suggests that politics, civil liberties concerns, and possible gaps in effectiveness preclude establishing a domestic in-

---

25. "Intelligence Shuffle," *Washington Post*, July 4, 2005, p. A16.

telligence agency and therefore leave us with no alternative but to embrace the reorganization and hope forlornly for the best. That there might be political opposition (mainly from the FBI itself) to creating such an agency is not a reason for not trying to create it but a prediction that the effort may fail. The effort might still be worthwhile in order to lay the groundwork for future reform. The civil liberties concerns are specious, as we shall see; and why creating another agency should open rather than close gaps is implausible and unexplained. Mindful that the reorganization may fail, the editorial wisely recommends that an "ongoing eye" be kept on the project but ignores the critical question of determining when "the end of the day" has come at which to pronounce the experiment a success or a failure. The longer that day of reckoning is postponed, the greater will be the gap between the need for domestic intelligence and the intelligence system's ability to meet that need.

Fearing infringements of civil liberties, the editorial writer urges that the collection of domestic intelligence be directed not by the President or "top administration officials" but by the FBI director "overseen by the attorney general." But the Attorney General *is* a "top administration official"; the FBI director is a police and security official rather than a civil libertarian; and if the National Security Service is directed by the FBI director rather than by the Director of National Intelligence, the goal of the reorganization—to create within the FBI a component of the overall intelligence system directed by the DNI—will be that much more difficult to reach.

3. A Better Solution

A new domestic intelligence agency is needed; but reform cannot stop there.

Coordination and Command

There are 17 federal intelligence agencies, scattered among different Cabinet-level departments, with the principal exception of the CIA, whose director reports to the President and the Director of National Intelligence rather than to a Cabinet member.[1] Before the Intelligence Reform Act, the different agencies, except those responsible for domestic intelligence (primarily the

---

1. The canonical figure for the number of separate agencies is 15, but is incomplete. There are five military intelligence agencies (one for each of the four uniformed services, plus the Defense Intelligence Agency), three technical intelligence agencies (the National Reconnaissance Office, the National Security Agency, and the National Geospatial-Imaging Agency), three domestic intelligence agencies (the FBI—treating its three intelligence-related divisions as one— plus two separate intelligence agencies in the Department of Homeland Security: the Directorate of Information Analysis and Infrastructure Protection and the Coast Guard's intelligence service); three foreign intelligence services (the CIA, the National Intelligence Council, and the State Department's Bureau of Intelligence and Research), and three that straddle domestic and foreign intelligence (the intelligence services of the Treasury and Energy departments and the National Counterterrorism Center). The NIC (National Intelligence Council) and the NCTC (National Counterterrorism Center), like the CIA, report to the President directly rather than to a department head. There will soon be an eighteenth intelligence agency—the National Counter Proliferation Center, authorized by the Intelligence Reform Act. On June 29, 2005, in the same memorandum directing the creation of the National Security Service, the President directed the DNI to establish the NCPC.

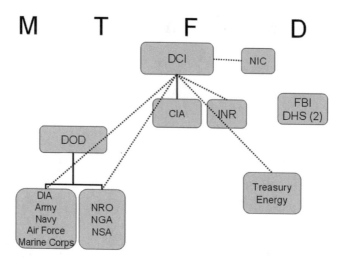

Fig. 1. The Intelligence System before the Intelligence Reform Act[2]

FBI), were loosely coordinated by the Director of Central Intelligence, who by law was also the Director of the CIA. The Intelligence Reform Act both separates the two jobholders and augments the duties and, less clearly, the powers of the Director of Central Intelligence, renaming the post "Director of National Intelligence."

Figure 1 depicts the structure of the intelligence system before the Act was passed, and Figure 2 the altered structure that the Act ordains. Solid lines indicate full control ("line authority"); broken lines indicate limited control, influence, general supervision, or coordination. The agencies can be divided roughly into four groups: from left to right in the two charts they

2. The acronyms in the charts, apart from those already familiar to the reader, are DIA (Defense Intelligence Agency), NRO (National Reconnaissance Office), NGA (National Geospatial-Intelligence Agency), NSA (National Security Agency), and INR (State Department Bureau of Intelligence and Research). The "2" after DHS in the charts signifies the two intelligence agencies within the Department of Homeland Security; actually the picture is more complex, as explained in the text below.

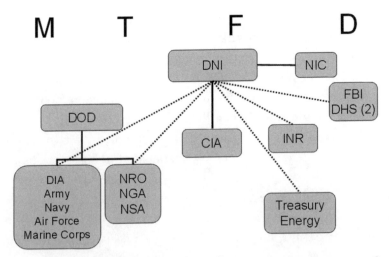

Fig. 2. The Intelligence System after the Intelligence Reform Act[2]

are military intelligence (labeled "M"), technical intelligence (T), foreign intelligence (F), and domestic intelligence (I), with the intelligence services of the Treasury and Energy departments, plus the National Intelligence Council, straddling the foreign-domestic divide. Omitted from the charts for the sake of simplicity is the National Counterterrorism Center (created by Presidential executive order in August of 2004), which includes representatives from the other intelligence agencies as well as its own staff and thus, before the Intelligence Reform Act, provided the only formal linkage between foreign and domestic intelligence.

The absence of effective coordination between domestic intelligence and foreign intelligence and among the various agencies involved in domestic intelligence was a weakness of the old regime. International terrorists operate both outside and inside the United States, moving back and forth across our porous borders.[3] The tracking of these terrorists requires close cooperation

3. By emphasizing international terrorism, I do not mean to depreciate the

among the CIA, the FBI, local police forces, private companies (including security consulting firms), and various agencies now lodged in the Department of Homeland Security. The necessary cooperation was impeded because the Director of Central Intelligence lacked authority over domestic intelligence, a deficiency remedied by the Intelligence Reform Act.

But to dismantle a barrier to cooperation is not to assure cooperation. The Director of National Intelligence should appoint a deputy for domestic intelligence to coordinate the domestic intelligence services[4] with each other and with the other federal intelligence services.[5] Such an official will be particularly needful if a domestic intelligence agency separate from the FBI is created, because, as we know, the agency and the Bureau must work closely together and there is bound to be resistance on the Bureau's side.

I must be more precise about what "coordination" entails. It cannot mean just calling meetings at which representatives of different agencies give their views, the coordinator decides what should be done—and the agencies treat his decision as nonbinding advice. Effective coordination requires a measure of command authority—the power to compel the sharing of information by requiring the different agencies to adopt compatible information technology and standards for access to each other's data-

---

potential threat posed by homegrown terrorists; the prospect of a biological Unabomber, for example, is terrifying.

4. It is an open question whether the authority of such an official should extend to the Treasury and Energy intelligence services, which conduct both domestic and foreign intelligence, though of a limited and specialized character.

5. The DNI has already used up the four deputy slots authorized to him by Congress—and the Intelligence Reform Act is explicit that "there may be not more than four Deputy Directors of National Intelligence." Intelligence Reform and Terrorism Prevention Act of 2004, § 1011(a), adding section 103A(b) to the National Security Act of 1947. The President may have inherent authority to create another deputyship. (I discuss his inherent authority over national security in the text below.) Anyway the title is not critical, since the Intelligence Reform Act authorizes the DNI to appoint "other . . . officials." Id., § 103(c)(9).

bases, and the power to create and supervise the necessary interagency intelligence task forces, establish an integrated national intelligence network of federal, state, local, and private intelligence services, and forge links to the other parts of the federal intelligence community. Command authority is not line authority, however; the employees of the intelligence agencies would not become employees of the Office of the Director of National Intelligence.

The agencies that do domestic intelligence are quite different from one another. This is obvious in the case of the Coast Guard, the Treasury Department, and the Department of Energy, but it is also true of DHS's other intelligence agency (besides the Coast Guard)—the Information Analysis Division in the Directorate of Information Analysis and Infrastructure Protection.[6] The division mainly gathers warning intelligence, assesses it, either declassifies it or scrubs the classified portions from it, and communicates threat warnings based on it to state and local agencies, such as police departments, that are in a position to prevent, or mitigate the effects of, an attack. The division also does some conventional intelligence analysis. The work of the division needs to be carefully integrated with the collection and analytical activities of the FBI and the other intelligence agencies. There are also, as we'll see, other intelligence units in the Department of Homeland Security. The task of coordinating all the nation's domestic intelligence assets is a formidable one, which should not be left to chance.

A New Agency

Chapters 1 and 2 of this monograph demonstrated that the FBI's intelligence failures have been serious, are inherent in confiding

6. The other and larger division in the Directorate—the Infrastructure Protection Division—assesses the vulnerability of potential terrorist targets. The Directorate is to be broken up as part of the reorganization of DHS discussed below.

domestic intelligence responsibility to a criminal investigation agency, and will not be cured by the consolidation of the Bureau's three intelligence-related divisions. In elaborating these points I presented most of the reasons for creating a domestic intelligence agency outside the FBI. The Bureau is well aware of these reasons, and its resistance to the proposal for consolidation was due in part to fear that it might be the prelude to lifting domestic intelligence right out of the Bureau, which would be easier to do with all the Bureau's intelligence assets in one place. The fear may be realistic—recall how the security service of the Royal Canadian Mounted Police was lifted out of the RCMP and made its own separate agency. But it would be a mistake to create a U.S. domestic intelligence agency in that fashion. Apart from points made earlier, we don't have enough domestic intelligence officers. We need more (and better), and forming a new agency would be an opportunity to obtain them. In contrast, rapid expansion of the FBI in the midst of its reorganization would be a recipe for disaster.

Although the total personnel of the five federal agencies with primarily domestic intelligence responsibilities (the FBI, the two intelligence agencies in DHS, and the intelligence units of the Treasury and Energy Departments) is not a published figure, it probably does not exceed 7,000, of whom probably no more than 5,000 are in the FBI.[7] Remarkably, MI5, though tiny (2,000

---

7. A recent audit report on the FBI by the Justice Department's Office of the Inspector General, *The Internal Effects of the Federal Bureau of Investigation's Reprioritization*, exh. 2-6 (Audit Report 04-39, Sept. 2004), www.usdoj.gov/oig/reports/FBI/a0439/final.pdf, reveals that 2,811 of the FBI's agents assigned to field offices are engaged in terrorism-related work. About 200 headquarters agents are also engaged in such work, and about 500 headquarters support staff are engaged in counterterrorism and counterintelligence activities (computed from exh. 2-11). If the number of field support staff is proportional to the number of field agents, this would imply that there are about 4,000 support personnel in the field offices who are supporting counterterrorism (calculated from exh. 2-2). That makes a total of some 7,500 (roughly a quarter of the entire staff of the FBI), but overstates the number of FBI employees engaged in domestic intelligence; for many of the

employees), is almost 30 percent the size of the U.S. domestic intelligence community, although the United States has more than four times the population of the United Kingdom and much less control over its borders yet faces graver, more varied, and more numerous threats. Even more striking is the fact that the Canadian Security Intelligence Service also has 2,000 employees. Although its population is much smaller than the United Kingdom's, its much greater land area is thought to require additional staff;[8] the inhabited land area of the United States is much greater than that of Canada.

Creating a new agency without displacing the intelligence element of the FBI would secure any efficiencies that FBI intelligence may be able to achieve by virtue of the Bureau's relations with local police forces, its experience in terrorist prosecutions— for that matter, its experience, checkered as it is, in national security intelligence—and the occasional overlaps of terrorist activity with ordinary crime. The need is to supplement the

---

analysts are engaged in ordinary-crimes intelligence and many of the special agents are engaged in criminal investigations of terrorist activities. I am guessing that only two-thirds—5,000—of the 7,500 are engaged in "pure" domestic intelligence, and this may well be an overestimate. As I noted in the text, moreover, much of the Bureau's counterterrorism activity, even some of its counterintelligence activity, may be concerned with only minor threats to national security.

Another and probably more accurate method of estimation proceeds from three rules of thumb used by the Bureau: ratio of intelligence special agents to intelligence analysts (2 to 1), of special agents to support staff (1 to .66), and of intelligence analysts to support staff (1 to .34). Then if (from the preceding paragraph) roughly 3,011 special agents (field, 2,811, plus headquarters, 200—the latter, however, a rough estimate) are engaged in intelligence-related work, there are 1,506 intelligence analysts, 1,987 special-agent support staff (3,011 × .66), and 512 intelligence-analyst support staff (1,506 × .34), for a grand total of 7,016, which is slightly lower than my previous estimate. Again, it is a substantial overestimate of "pure" national security intelligence personnel, because it includes special agents assigned to counterterrorism prosecutions and intelligence analysts assigned either to such prosecutions or to ordinary-crimes intelligence.

8. David Collins, "Spies Like Them: The Canadian Security Intelligence Service and Its Place in World Intelligence," 24 *Sydney Law Review* 505, 512 (2002).

Bureau's intelligence components with a new agency that will have a distinctive focus and culture, not to break up the Bureau.

But although the FBI should continue to play a major role in federal intelligence liaison with local police, a domestic intelligence agency could play an equal or even more important role. The rivalries among law enforcement agencies are acute because of competition for funds, overlapping authority, different cultures, the FBI's traditional hauteur, and fear of a rival agency's "stealing" one's cases. Many local law enforcers feel deserted by the federal government in general, and the FBI in particular, in regard to national security intelligence. The Bureau does not treat them as its partners or even its customers. FBI agents have been known to brush off attempts by local police, and even by other federal officers, to obtain the Bureau's aid in intelligence matters.[9] I am told that the FBI turned down an offer of a simple computer-communications system that would have linked the

9. Here is a typical anecdote. I cannot vouch for, but have no reason to doubt, its accuracy. A customs officer stopped a truck driver who was crossing the border from Canada to the United States. The driver appeared to be of Arab ethnicity and had a license to carry hazmat (hazardous materials), although the load he was carrying on this occasion did not include any such materials. In conversation with the officer, the driver described himself as a "salifist." The officer called the special agent in charge of the nearest FBI field office and asked him what the word meant. The agent replied that unless the customs officer was planning to make an arrest, he (the agent) wasn't interested in answering the officer's questions. In fact, "salifist" or "salafist" is a term used by radical Islamists to denote a person who believes in the fundamental beliefs of Mohammad. Although members of al Qaeda call themselves salifists, not all salifists are terrorists. But a truck driver crossing a border into the United States who has a license to carry hazmat merits careful scrutiny. An intelligence-minded officer would either have answered the customs officer's question or told him "I don't know but I'll find out and get back to you." A Google search would have yielded a serviceable answer within seconds.

I recognize the limited probative value of anecdotage. A thorough study of the FBI's relations to local law enforcement in regard to national security intelligence would be an excellent project for the Justice Department's Inspector General, the General Accountability Office, congressional oversight committees, or the Office of the Director of National Intelligence.

Joint Terrorism Task Forces directly to squad cars so that police officers could send and receive timely information concerning possible terrorist activities.

A domestic intelligence agency not linked to any law enforcement agency would stand above the fray and be trusted as an honest broker—especially if it were authorized to reimburse some of the intelligence-related costs of state and local law enforcement agencies, such as costs of information technology, of training intelligence officers, and of paying informants. In effect, the domestic intelligence agency would be buying intelligence data from the many police departments that, with proper incentives, can gather abundant data. The agency would be in a good position to take the lead in creating the coordinated nationwide intelligence network that we need and don't have.

An initial way to fulfill the lead role might be for members of the agency's staff to visit all 20,000 state and local police forces. That would not be so formidable an undertaking as it may seem; 200 officers, each visiting two police forces a week, could complete the project in a year. The visits, and follow-up communications, would be intended, along with short training programs for those police officers (usually in the larger cities) who are actually assigned to do intelligence work, to indicate activities and persons that the police should be on the alert for, and on how and with whom in the agency the police should exchange information.

As a new entrant to the intelligence scene, a domestic intelligence agency separate from the FBI would be in a good position to experiment with improved intelligence practices, such as a shorter replacement cycle for information technology, greater receptivity to commercial off-the-shelf technology, greater use of statistical and economic techniques for prioritization (such as cost-benefit analysis), greater reliance on open-source materials, more flexible hiring practices, and increased investment in artificial-intelligence aids to translation and data analysis.

The idea of creating a U.S. domestic intelligence agency is commonly called the "MI5 solution." MI5 is the best known of the foreign domestic intelligence agencies, and the United Kingdom is our closest ally. But a better model for a U.S. domestic intelligence agency from a public-relations standpoint (and the importance of good public relations for a domestic intelligence agency should not be underestimated, given civil liberties concerns and FBI opposition) is the Canadian domestic intelligence agency. MI5, throughout most of its long history, which began in 1909, operated without any judicial control. That would be unthinkable in the United States but seemed natural in the United Kingdom, which had no tradition of separation of powers. Violations of civil liberties were common.[10] Merely the use of a military acronym for a domestic intelligence agency ("MI" stands for "military intelligence")—even though MI5 has long been a civilian agency—strikes an ominous note. The Canadian Security Intelligence Service (CSIS),[11] though modeled on MI5, does not have these drawbacks. It has no military origins or overtones and is subject to an elaborate set of controls[12] designed to prevent it from infringing civil liberties.

10. See, for example, Center for Democracy and Technology, "Domestic Intelligence Agencies: The Mixed Record of the UK's MI5" 3–6 (Jan. 27, 2003).

11. I quote its mission statement in the appendix. Two of the missions assigned to CSIS are conducting background investigations of applicants for government employment and screening immigrants. These are intelligence, rather than law enforcement, functions that in the United States are currently lodged in the FBI and in DHS's Immigration and Customs Enforcement agency, respectively. They could be transferred to a domestic intelligence agency, but that is a peripheral issue that I shall not try to resolve.

12. See the CSIS home page under "Accountability and Review," at www.csis-scrs.gc.ca/eng/backgrnd/back2_e.html; also Daniel Cuyley Chung, "Internal Security: Establishment of a Canadian Security Intelligence Service," 26 *Harvard International Law Journal* 234 (1985).

CSIS cannot be a complete model for a U.S. domestic intelligence agency. There are too many differences, particularly in population and perceived threats, between the United States and Canada. And I cannot vouch for the adequacy of CSIS's funding or the quality of its management, its personnel, or its operational methods.[13] But the concept and basic design of the agency provide an attractive template for a U.S. domestic intelligence agency. The history of CSIS is, moreover, further evidence of the need for our own SIS. It was dissatisfaction with the performance of the Royal Canadian Mounted Police—the Canadian counterpart of the FBI—in domestic intelligence that prompted the creation of CSIS.[14]

Siting the New Agency: The DHS Option

So we need a new agency outside the FBI. But where outside? It could be a stand-alone like the CIA—that is, not part of any Cabinet-level department—reporting to the DNI as the CIA now does except for covert operations (the CIA reports on those directly to the President), which anyway would not be a proper activity for a domestic intelligence agency.[15] But fear of empowering the President to spy on his political enemies in the manner

13. For criticism, see "Epidemic of Espionage," *Newsbeat 1*, June 19, 2005, newsbeat1.com/2005/06/epidemic-of-espionage.html.

14. Chung, note 12 above, at 235.

15. The term "covert operations" refers to operations, often involving physical force, which because of their illegality or violation of moral principles are considered permissible only when used against foreigners in foreign countries, and even then must be kept in deep enough secrecy to enable the President and other policymakers to plausibly deny knowledge of the operations. An intelligence agency would not be permitted to use such tactics on American soil, though it would be permitted to use methods of surveillance and penetration lawfully used in criminal investigations, and nonviolent disruptive activities such as disinformation and other deceptive practices, exposure, and bribery, subject to appropriate safeguards to ensure the protection of privacy, free speech, and other legal rights.

of Nixon's "plumbers" argues for lodging such an agency instead in a department, so that there is a Cabinet officer who is not himself an intelligence officer between the agency and the President. The Department of Homeland Security is the logical choice. Locating the agency there would conform to the practice of foreign nations. For example, MI5 reports to the Home Secretary, who corresponds to our Secretary of Homeland Security, and the director of the Canadian Security Intelligence Service reports to the Minister for Public Safety and Emergency Preparedness. The planned reorganization of DHS announced recently by Secretary Chertoff will, as we'll see, simplify the creation of a domestic intelligence agency within the department.

Locating the agency in DHS would have the following advantages besides interposing an official who is not an intelligence official between the agency and the President:

1. Unlike the FBI, DHS has no J. Edgar Hoover legacy. This should further reassure civil libertarians.

2. The coordination of DHS's immense information sources—including Immigration and Customs Enforcement, the Transportation Security Administration, the Border Patrol, and the Secret Service—would be facilitated. These agencies take in an enormous amount of information every day, much of which may have value to an intelligence agency. A domestic intelligence agency within DHS would have readier access to this information than an outside agency would.

3. The agencies mentioned in the preceding paragraph are all "prevention" agencies, just as DHS as a whole is a prevention department. Intelligence fits better with prevention than with prosecution. Think how closely related inspecting cargo for radioactivity (prevention) is to collecting information on persons who have tried to obtain radioactive materials for questionable purposes (intelligence). The preventers will be obtaining information that the intelligence agency wants, and vice versa.

Stated otherwise, placing a domestic intelligence agency in DHS would bring domestic intelligence closer to its customers. An agency responsible for preventing dangerous cargoes from entering U.S. ports wants to know what ports, shippers, carriers, types of ship, crewmembers, longshoremen, etc. to concentrate on—just the sort of information that a domestic intelligence agency would want to have. Separating domestic intelligence from prevention of domestic attacks is like taking military intelligence out of the armed forces, and is objectionable for the same reason: it separates the suppliers of intelligence from their principal customers.[16]

4. If sited in DHS, the new agency, though genuinely new, would not be starting from scratch. It would build on the Information Analysis Division and on the Coast Guard's intelligence service, both of which are members of the intelligence community, and also on intelligence units in other DHS agencies; these include the field intelligence units of Immigration and Customs Enforcement, the field intelligence center in the Border Patrol, and some of the very able intelligence specialists in the Secret Service. Incorporating these intelligence units,[17] along with the Coast Guard's intelligence service, into the new agency[18] would answer any complaint that we have enough intelligence agencies already and shouldn't create another one. Since the Information

16. Cf. John Deutch, "The Smart Approach to Intelligence," *Washington Post*, Sept. 9, 2002, p. A17.

17. The suggestion is not to reduce the resources that the Secret Service devotes to the protection of the President and others whom the service protects, but to divert some of the intelligence capabilities that tend between Presidential election campaigns (which is when the service's protective duties are most extensive) to be devoted to counterfeiting, cellphone fraud, and other crimes unrelated to protection.

18. Intelligence personnel from the Coast Guard would remain Coast Guard service members. They would merely be detailed to the new agency, just as members of the armed services are detailed to the National Security Agency, a large fraction of whose staff is military.

Analysis Division and the Coast Guard's intelligence service are two of the existing 17 (soon to be 18) federal intelligence agencies, were they both incorporated into a domestic intelligence agency the total number of intelligence agencies would fall by one. Anyway the idea that 17 or 18 is "too many" intelligence agencies is unsupported. Think of them as the 18 divisions of a $40 billion company with 100,000 employees; it is not an excessive number.

5. Although the size of the Department of Homeland Security may seem to argue against placing still another agency in it, there would be offsetting advantages. The department is large enough that it should be possible to relocate a sufficient number of its employees to free up the necessary office space for the new agency (although secure and hardened office space is actually rather scarce in the department). The department could also provide basic administrative staff and seed money, and in this and other ways shorten the period necessary for the new agency to become fully operational. Indeed, at a guess the total annual budget of the new agency would not exceed $250 million (above the amount the department now spends on intelligence), which is only two-thirds of 1 percent of the department's total budget and so might be financed by cuts elsewhere in it; in that event no net increase in appropriations would be required.

Two disadvantages of the DHS siting option should be noted. The first is that the department is still suffering from acute growing pains; working for DHS is not considered a good way of polishing one's résumé. But this disadvantage can be overcome by stressing the autonomy of the new agency. The Secret Service has not lost its prestige by being transferred from the Treasury Department to DHS, even though the Treasury Department is the more prestigious department.

A related disadvantage concerns the bureaucratic structure

of DHS. There is an Undersecretary for Information Analysis and Infrastructure Protection but also an Assistant Secretary for Information Analysis, and it is the latter whom the Intelligence Reform Act designates as the head of DHS intelligence. To place the new agency under that assistant secretary, who in turn reports to the undersecretary, would unduly complicate the command/control structure (for remember that all federal intelligence agencies now also report to the DNI).

This problem, however, will be solved by the reorganization announced by Secretary Chertoff. Here are the key passages from his speech announcing it:

> The fact is that systematic intelligence lies at the heart of everything that we do. Understanding the enemy's intent and capabilities affects how we operate at our borders, how we assess risk in protecting infrastructure, how we discern the kind of threats for which we must be prepared to respond.
>
> Right now, there are more than 10 separate components or offices of the Department of Homeland Security, which are intelligence generators, and all of us in the Department are consumers and users of intelligence information. We need to have a common picture across this Department, of the intelligence that we generate and the intelligence that we require. We need to fuse that information and combine it with information from other members of the intelligence community, as well as information from our state and local and international partners.
>
> And as I said earlier, DHS can also do a better job of sharing the intelligence we're gathering and the intelligence we're analyzing with our customers inside the Department, with the intelligence community as a whole, and with our frontline first responders at the state and local level.
>
> Therefore, today, I am announcing that the Assistant Secretary for Information Analysis will be designated as the Chief Intelligence Officer for the Department of Homeland Security. The Chief Intelligence Officer will head a strengthened Intelli-

gence and Analysis division that will report directly to me. This office will ensure that intelligence is coordinated, fused and analyzed within the Department so that we have a common operational picture of what's going on. It will also provide a primary connection between DHS and the intelligence community as a whole, and a primary source of information for state, local and private sector partners.[19]

Thus, under the reorganization the Assistant Secretary for Information Analysis—who would be the logical person to head up a domestic intelligence agency within the Department—will be reporting directly to the Secretary of Homeland Security, a welcome simplification of the command structure. Also welcome is the fact that he will be in charge of all intelligence in the Department, and hence of the intelligence units of the Coast Guard, Immigration and Customs Enforcement, and the other agencies in the department. The Office of Information and Analysis could thus be the nucleus of a Security Intelligence Service. The nucleus—not the service itself, because it will have, if one may judge from Secretary Chertoff's description (which may be abbreviated), no operating officers. Also, though this may seem a trivial point, from a recruiting standpoint "Office of Intelligence and Analysis" is not a good name for an elite, autonomous intelligence agency; it has no pizzazz. (The logical name for the agency would be "Security Intelligence Service.") Nevertheless, the reorganization could be the first step to the creation of a genuine, "full service" domestic intelligence agency.

The head of the agency could double as the DNI's deputy for domestic intelligence if such a deputy were to be appointed. The 9/11 Commission had proposed that the chief intelligence officer of either the Department of Homeland Security or the FBI be dual hatted as the DNI's deputy for domestic intelligence.

19. Michael Chertoff, "Second Stage Review Remarks," July 13, 2005, www .dhs.gov/dhspublic/interapp/speech/speech_0255.xml.

Giving the same person line authority over the domestic intelligence agency and coordination authority over the other elements of domestic intelligence would replicate the dual hatting of the CIA's director (remember that he was both DCI and DCIA), but it would do so on a much smaller, and therefore a manageable, scale. It would be a scale comparable to the dual hatting of the DNI's deputy for intelligence analysis, who doubles as the director of the National Intelligence Council.

Granted, competing agencies would fear that the dual hatter would favor "his" agency, in much the same way that the DCI was suspected of favoring the CIA and so encountered resistance to his efforts to manage the intelligence community as a whole. But it would probably be better on balance to have the same person both direct the new agency and be the DNI's deputy for domestic intelligence (and thus exercise, by delegation from the DNI, the command/coordination authority that I described earlier), at least in the early stages of the new agency. This would give the official greater clout in his dealings with the FBI (and he would need that) and also minimize friction and hierarchy.

Finding a Role; Relation to Other Agencies

The structure of the U.S. intelligence system that is emerging from the Intelligence Reform Act and its implementation by the Director of National Intelligence may seem to leave no room for a domestic intelligence agency separate from the newly hatched (or hatching) National Security Service and the specialized intelligence services of Homeland Security, Energy, and Treasury. The Director of National Intelligence has deputies for analysis and collection, not limited to foreign intelligence, while the National Counterterrorism Center (NCTC) is flexing its muscles and has recently been described as "the nation's primary agency for analyzing terrorist threats and planning counterterrorism operations *at home* and abroad."[20]

What is left for a domestic intelligence agency to do? A *great* deal:

(a) collecting intelligence data directly, by human and technical means (and also from open-source materials),[21] within the United States, and doing so more adroitly than the FBI, handicapped by its criminal-investigation mentality, is capable of doing (the NCTC is not a collection agency);

(b) gathering such data indirectly from federal, state, local, and private agencies that collect or can be encouraged to collect intelligence data, including the prevention agencies within DHS, such as the Border Patrol, the Coast Guard, Immigration and Customs Enforcement, and the Transportation Security Administration;

(c) in support of (b), establishing through a training center, personal contacts, financial assistance, and a digitized communications system a nationwide network for the collection of domestic intelligence data;

(d) pooling the data collected directly and indirectly by the agency with data from other federal intelligence agencies (another job such an agency should be able to do better than the IT-challenged FBI) and with open-source data;

(e) sharing data with other intelligence agencies on demand (including the FBI, which would be an important customer);

(f) analyzing data and using the analyses together with analyses of infrastructure vulnerabilities to make threat assessments;

---

20. Walter Pincus, "Counterterrorism Center Awaits Presidential Action: Director and Chain of Command Are Needed by June 17," *Washington Post*, June 3, 2005, p. A21 (emphasis added).

21. Already being urged by Congressman Rob Simmons as an appropriate task for DHS. Caitlin Harrington, "Former CIA Man Simmons Shoots Again for Unclassified Intelligence Unit at DHS," *Congressional Quarterly*, June 22, 2005, www.johnbatchelorshow.com/article.cfm?id=1170.

(g) issuing threat warnings to first responders and other concerned agencies;

(h) establishing cooperative counterterrorism relationships with the U.S. Arab and Muslim communities;

(i) conducting, through undercover officers and paid or otherwise induced informants, surveillance and penetration of suspected terrorist cells (not limited to cells of Islamic or other foreign terrorist groups), and of groups suspected of providing financial aid, recruits, information, or other assistance to terrorists;

(j) conducting the very limited, nonviolent disruption operations that would be proper for a domestic intelligence agency to conduct;[22]

(k) conducting counterintelligence, for example against attempted penetration of the agency itself, or other components of the Department of Homeland Security, by agents of terrorist groups or of foreign states.

All this would be done under the general supervision of both the Office of the Director of National Intelligence and the National Counterterrorism Center, except that the NCTC is prohibited by the Intelligence Reform Act from analyzing and integrating "intelligence pertaining exclusively to domestic terrorists,"[23] that is, homegrown terrorists, though these are a major potential threat. So here is a yawning gap for a domestic intelligence agency to fill. But with that exception, the ability of the director of the domestic intelligence agency to initiate timely intelligence operations, whether to collect intelligence or to disrupt terrorist plots, may be impaired by his having to obtain clearances from multiple levels of higher authority—a formula for delay and for diffusion of responsibility. Were the head of a new

22. Note 15 above.
23. Intelligence Reform and Terrorism Prevention Act of 2004, § 1021, adding section 119(d)(1), to the National Security Act of 1947.

domestic intelligence agency to be a different person from the deputy DNI for domestic intelligence, this would add another layer of control; so here is another argument for the dual hatting that I have suggested.

Getting Started

The system of domestic intelligence sketched above could be largely or perhaps even entirely created by Presidential executive order. The largest of the nation's intelligence agencies, the National Security Agency, was created by Presidential executive order rather than by an Act of Congress.[24] Most U.S. intelligence services were first created that way, a recent example being the creation in August 2004 of the National Counterterrorism Center.[25] Even an order by the Secretary of Homeland Security might suffice to transform the department's Office of Intelligence and Analysis (successor to the Information Analysis Division) into a full-fledged domestic intelligence agency, much as the Defense Intelligence Agency was created by order of the Secretary of Defense.

24. *The Intelligence Community: History, Organization, and Issues* 351 (statement of Lt. Gen. Lew Allen Jr., Director, National Security Agency), 519 (Tyrus G. Fain, ed., 1977). See also John D. Bansemer, "Intelligence Reform: A Question of Balance" (Harvard University Center for Information Policy Research, Program on Information Resources Policy, Apr. 18, 2005), http://pirp.harvard.edu/pubs_pdf/banseme/banseme-draft-05.pdf, at 36, describing significant changes in the organization of the intelligence system made in 1972 by President Nixon without congressional authorization. For helpful introductions to the legal issues mentioned in the text, see Russell J. Bruemmer, "Intelligence Community Reorganization: Declining the Invitation to Struggle," 101 *Yale Law Journal* 867 (1992); David Everett Colton, Comment, "Speaking Truth to Power: Intelligence Oversight in an Imperfect World," 137 *University of Pennsylvania Law Review* 571 (1988).

25. On the scope of the authority that Presidents have exercised through executive orders and cognate devices, see Phillip J. Cooper, *By Order of the President: The Use and Abuse of Executive Direct Action* (2002).

It is even possible that a domestic intelligence agency could be created by the Director of National Intelligence by interpretation of the Intelligence Reform Act. Take so trivial-seeming a provision of that Act as "the Director of National Intelligence shall ensure the elimination of waste and unnecessary duplication within the intelligence community."[26] This seems a fatuous exhortation. Yet on the plausible theory that legislation, like the Constitution itself, implicitly confers on an agency the powers "necessary and proper" to enable it to fulfill the duties expressly imposed upon it by the legislation, the provision could be interpreted to authorize the DNI to exercise such authority as may be necessary (required) and proper (lawful) to eliminate waste and unnecessary duplication.

In any event, the authority conferred on the President by Article II of the Constitution to command the armed forces and direct foreign policy, and thus to take charge of national defense and national security, of which intelligence was a recognized component long before the drafting of the Constitution,[27] should empower the President to create, combine, separate, and reconfigure components of the intelligence system without congressional authorization. Conceivably his authority in these respects may not even be subject to congressional override, beyond what is implicit in Congress's control of the federal budget. And what is implicit in that control may be less than what we have become accustomed to. "As President of the United States from 1789 to 1797, [George] Washington took personal responsibility for foreign intelligence. . . . Congress required him to certify what sums he had spent, but allowed him to conceal both the purposes and

26. Intelligence Reform and Terrorism Prevention Act of 2004, § 1011(a), adding section 102(a)(f)(5) to the National Security Act of 1947.

27. It is on a similar theory that the President's power to authorize covert operations by the CIA has been found in Article II. *The Intelligence Community*, note 24 above, at 9.

recipients of payments from the fund."[28] Domestic intelligence may seem too sensitive a subject for the President to assert control over without congressional authorization. But, if so, Congress has made clear in the Intelligence Reform Act that it *wants* domestic intelligence to be an integrated component of the intelligence community administered by the President and his subordinate officials.

Questions of legal authority to one side, the creation of a new national security agency (other than by the simple combinatorial method that is giving us the National Security Service) may seem a daunting undertaking. But that depends on the size of the agency, on the degree to which its operation depends on complex and expensive technologies, and, as I have emphasized, on where it is placed in the government structure. Given the existence of other federal domestic intelligence agencies (for remember that I am not suggesting curtailment of the FBI's intelligence operations), the aid in collection, analysis, and technical services that the new agency would receive from other federal intelligence agencies, and the intelligence resources of the nation's numerous police forces both public and private, the new agency would not have to be large. And its only major nonpersonnel expenses would be the rent of secured and hardened office space and the purchase of communications equipment and computer hardware and software

A total staff as small as 1,500, beyond the existing intelligence personnel in the Department of Homeland Security, might suffice, certainly at the start. An agency of such modest dimensions might, under forceful leadership, be operational within a few months because placing it in DHS would facilitate a prompt launch.

28. Christopher Andrew, *For the President's Eyes Only: Secret Intelligence and the American Presidency from Washington to Bush* 11 (1995).

Civil Liberties

Any strengthening of domestic intelligence capabilities is bound to draw complaints from civil liberties advocates because surveillance of groups and individuals gives rise to concerns about possible infringements of privacy and of freedom of speech. In evaluating such complaints, one must separate two issues. One is where to draw the boundary between security and liberty concerns, a question that I have addressed elsewhere.[29] Here I will merely note two points concerning that boundary-drawing issue: that the public safety is as much a constitutional value as personal liberty is, and that security and liberty are inseparable because another terrorist attack on the scale of 9/11 would be the greatest possible setback to civil liberties in the United States, since the reflex reaction—we saw it after 9/11—to such an attack is to curtail those liberties.[30]

The other issue is whether, wherever the line is drawn, a domestic intelligence agency is likely to cross it. The agency should not cross it because that would be illegal and expose the agency's personnel to civil and even criminal sanctions; no agency is exempt from the Constitution and laws of the United States. Probably the agency would not cross the line in any event because to do so would be profoundly imprudent from the agency's own standpoint. Given the civil liberties concerns to which the creation of such an agency would give rise, and the fragility of any new, small agency, any infraction of constitutional liberties could well doom the experiment. Moreover, the last thing a domestic intelligence agency would want to do would be

29. Posner, note 6 above, at 185–196; Richard A. Posner, *Catastrophe: Risk and Return* 224–243 (2004); Richard A. Posner, *Law, Pragmatism, and Democracy* 293–317 (2003).

30. See, for example, Alan Cowell, "British Seek New Laws to Confront Terror," *New York Times* (national ed.), July 18, 2005, p. A8.

to alienate the large Arab and Muslim communities in the United States by infringing the civil liberties of their members. The agency would depend critically on their cooperation in informing on any terrorists or terrorist sympathizers in their midst; and if they became disaffected to the point of actively assisting terrorist activities, the nation's terrorist problem would be compounded enormously. That is a lesson of the recent suicide bombings in London, which were carried out by British citizens.

Moreover, from the standpoint of civil liberties the overall scale of domestic intelligence activity is more important than how that activity is parceled out among different agencies. To the extent that domestic intelligence places pressure on civil liberties, that pressure is greater the more domestic intelligence officers there are. But the number is going to grow, one way or another, because domestic intelligence is undermanned. Whether it grows by expansion of the FBI or by creating a brand-new agency or by expanding the intelligence capabilities of the Department of Homeland Security is probably unrelated to the ultimate number, though if anything the former route will conduce to a greater overall growth in domestic intelligence—precisely because there is less opposition by civil libertarians to expanding the FBI than to creating a separate agency.

There should not be. It requires a lapse of historical memory to think that an FBI monopoly of domestic intelligence is a guarantee of respect for civil liberties. As revealed by the Church Committee, until the mid-1970s the FBI, despite being a part of the Justice Department and therefore nominally subordinate to the nation's chief legal officer, repeatedly committed serious infractions of civil liberties in pursuit (sometimes misguided) of its domestic intelligence mission, such as its relentless electronic surveillance of the private life of Martin Luther King Jr.[31]

31. The report of the Church Committee is *Intelligence Activities and the Rights of Americans: Final Report of the U.S. Senate Select Committee to Study Government Operations with Respect to Intelligence Activities*, bk. 2, S. Rep. No.

In fact, to quote Senator Richard Shelby, a domestic intelligence agency "might offer advantages over our current structure even in terms of civil liberties. . . . I suspect that most Americans . . . would feel safer having [domestic intelligence] collection performed by intelligence officers who do *not* possess coercive powers—and who can only actually take *action* against someone through a process of formal coordination with law enforcement officials."[32] Americans don't want someone whose job is to arrest and convict acting on what he imagines is going on in an individual's place of worship, business, or bedroom, but we do want those who are charged with protecting the country to look for indications that the individual is up to no good with that bioengineering equipment he's been shipping into the sacristy. "If we don't want a secret police, maybe we should put the secrets and the police in different agencies."[33]

The fear and indignation that the arrests of the two Muslim teenagers engendered in their families and ethnic community were augmented by their being imprisoned and the further fact that because the investigation was intelligence-related, the FBI, to protect its sources, could not give a full and convincing account of the reasons for its actions.[34] The priority of a domestic intelligence agency would be to construct cooperative relationships with members of the Muslim communities in the United States[35]—not on making arrests in those communities, which has

755, 94th Cong., 2d Sess. (1976). For a summary of its findings, see *The Intelligence Community*, note 24 above, ch. 12.

32. "September 11 and the Imperative of Reform in the U.S. Intelligence Community: Additional Views of Senator Richard C. Shelby, Vice Chairman, Senate Select Committee on Intelligence," Dec. 10, 2002, p. 75, www.fas.org/irp/congress/2002_rpt/shelby.pdf.

33. Stuart Taylor Jr., "Spying on Terrorists," *Government Executive*, Jan. 13, 2003, www.govexec.com/dailyfed/0103/011303ff.htm.

34. Nina Bernstein, "Questions, Bitterness and Exile for Queens Girl in Terror Case," *New York Times* (national ed.), June 17, 2005, pp. A1, A20.

35. That is why a domestic intelligence agency must have operating officers, though they cannot be anywhere near as freewheeling as CIA operating officers.

been the focus of the Joint Terrorism Task Forces, dominated by the FBI.

There is a history of the FBI's redefining criminal investigations as intelligence operations in order to use FISA warrants and NSA intercepts to obtain information for use in drug or other ordinary-crimes investigations.[36] This bothers civil libertarians. It would not be a temptation for a domestic intelligence agency, the only concern of which would be national security.

In arguing that the FBI's lodgment in the Justice Department sensitizes the Bureau to civil liberties, civil libertarians ignore the opposite possibility—that the FBI's growing involvement in intelligence will desensitize the Department to civil liberties. Would civil libertarians want an intelligence officer to be appointed Attorney General or Deputy Attorney General because the FBI had given priority to intelligence?

Europeans, who believe that in the USA Patriot Act and elsewhere the United States has gone too far in curtailing civil liberties because of fears for national security, consider their approach of separating domestic intelligence from law enforcement to be less invasive of civil liberties than the American approach, with its emphasis on arrest and prosecution that results from the FBI's paramount role in domestic intelligence. Despite the recent bombings in London (which prove merely that no police or intelligence system can provide a 100 percent guaranty against terrorist attacks), British "intelligence has been very good at keeping tabs on Muslim radicals inside Britain and has succeeded in foiling earlier terrorist plots. 'MI5 has very good relations with the British Muslim community, and it's developed a good network of informants, and they've penetrated the radical groups.'"[37] The British may well be placing insufficient emphasis

36. Stewart A. Baker, "Should Spies Be Cops?" *Foreign Policy*, Dec. 22, 1994, p. 36.

37. Richard Bernstein, "Rights vs. Security: Despite Terror, Europeans Seem Determined to Maintain Civil Liberties," *New York Times* (national ed.), July 9, 2005, p. A8.

on police methods to combat terrorism,[38] but my point is only that they correctly perceive less tension between MI5-style domestic intelligence and civil liberties than between police measures and civil liberties.

Civil libertarians thus are wrong to think that because the FBI is part of the Justice Department it is less likely to infringe civil liberties than a domestic intelligence agency would be. They may be on somewhat firmer ground in thinking that the Bureau's concern that the prosecutions it assists stand up in court makes it more fastidious about avoiding rights violations that would jeopardize a conviction than an agency having no law enforcement responsibilities would be. But this fastidiousness will carry over to the Bureau's pure intelligence activities only if the Bureau is indeed unable to shake off its culture of law enforcement— and if it is unable to do that it will be ineffectual in the intelligence role.

One wonders whether the real reason that civil libertarians want the FBI to continue to dominate domestic intelligence is that to the extent that the Bureau's conduct of intelligence is ineffectual the threat to civil liberties is reduced (though the threat to public safety is increased). This suspicion is supported by the chorus of civil liberties complaints that greeted the announcement of the creation of the National Security Service.[39] The NSS is not intended to expand the FBI's intelligence operations or to give the Bureau additional powers, but merely to make those operations more effective.

If no domestic intelligence agency is created, and if the FBI, preoccupied with its reorganization, does not expand its intelli-

38. Elaine Sciolino and Don Van Natta Jr., "For a Decade, London Thrived as a Busy Crossroads of Terror," *New York Times* (final national ed.), July 10, 2005, §1, p. 1.

39. Dan Eggen and Walter Pincus, "Spy Chief Gets More Authority over FBI: Negroponte Will Control Bureau's Intelligence Side," *Washington Post*, June 30, 2005, p. A1.

gence staff rapidly, other agencies will rush in to fill the void; for as I have said, there is a shortage of domestic intelligence officers—and government abhors a bureaucratic vacuum. The Pentagon is one such agency. Already it is moving to expand its role in domestic security, including domestic intelligence.[40] Is *this* what civil libertarians want?

What is important from the standpoint of protecting civil liberties is not that domestic intelligence be controlled by the FBI but that it be subject to legal and administrative controls intelligently designed to check abuses. There are many possibilities, quite apart from the measures legislated in the Intelligence Reform Act (the creation of the position of Civil Liberties Protection Officer in the Office of the DNI and the creation of a Privacy and Civil Liberties Oversight Board in the Executive Office of the President):

(a) lodging the new agency in the Department of Homeland Security, so that, as I mentioned earlier, there would be an official who was not an intelligence officer between the agency and the White House;

(b) creating a domestic intelligence oversight board composed primarily of lawyers with civil liberties expertise;

(c) assigning special oversight responsibilities for domestic intelligence to the Privacy and Civil Liberties Oversight Board;

(d) subjecting the domestic intelligence agency to the guidelines promulgated by the Attorney General to regulate the FBI's intelligence operations;

(e) creating a steering committee for the agency composed of the Attorney General, the Director of National Intelligence, and the Secretary of Homeland Security;

(f) incorporating controls similar to those that Canada has placed on CSIS;

40. Bradley Graham, "Military Expands Homeland Efforts: Pentagon to Share Data with Civilian Agencies," *Washington Post*, July 6, 2005, p. A1.

(g) suggesting that Congress lodge oversight responsibility for domestic intelligence either in the Senate Homeland Security and Government Affairs Committee (and its House counterpart)—which presumably would be the automatic consequence of placing the agency in the Department of Homeland Security—rather than in the intelligence committees;

(h) appointing as the agency's director someone from outside the intelligence and national security communities;

(i) limiting the jurisdiction of the new agency to the collection and analysis of intelligence relating to activities that threaten to cause *major* loss of life, or comparable harm to the public welfare (that is, defining national security narrowly).

Conclusion

Domestic intelligence in the United States today is undermanned, understudied, undersupervised, uncoordinated, technologi-
cally challenged, tied too closely to criminal law enforcement,
and (the same point, really) dominated by an agency (the FBI)
that, because its primary activity is law enforcement, is structur-
ally unsuited to play the central role in domestic national security
intelligence—and all this at a time of extreme danger and vulnerability. A terrorist who wants to enter the United States can
do so with relative ease either with forged documents or by being
smuggled across the Canadian or Mexican borders. The U.S.
government has to be able to find, follow, watch, overhear,
deceive, bribe, and expose (and not just arrest and prosecute)
suspected terrorists plus groups and individuals that assist them
by providing safe houses, financing, weapons, or other forms of
support. To this end it must collect and compare and analyze
masses of data concerning foreign visitors, plants where weapons
are made and stores where they are sold, laboratories where lethal
pathogens and toxins are stored, locations and shipments of
radioactive materials, potential targets, and much else besides.
Nor can the threat posed by homegrown terrorists in the era of
weapons of mass destruction be ignored.

Reorganizing the FBI cannot be the answer, given the deep
tension between criminal investigation and national security
intelligence. There is urgent need for a domestic intelligence
agency, modeled on the Canadian Security Intelligence Service,
that would be separate from the FBI and would have no authority

to engage in law enforcement. Such an agency would not draw staff from the FBI; the Bureau would retain its existing intelligence responsibilities and staff.

The recently announced reorganization of the Department of Homeland Security includes creation of a nascent domestic intelligence agency within the department; that nucleus should be expanded into a full-fledged Security Intelligence Service that would focus on (1) building cooperative relationships with the U.S. Muslim community in order to enlist its aid in detecting terrorist activity, (2) surveillance and penetration of suspected terrorist groups, and (3) creating a nationwide "eyes and ears" network of public officers on the alert for possible terrorist plans and acts The director of the Security Intelligence Service should be dual hatted by the Director of National Intelligence as his deputy for domestic intelligence. In that capacity he or she would be charged with coordinating all federal domestic intelligence services with each other and with the other intelligence services.

Appendix: Mission Statement of the Canadian Security Intelligence Service[1]

The Canadian Security Intelligence Service (CSIS) was created by an Act of Parliament in 1984, following the McDonald Commission of Inquiry in the late 1970s and the Mackenzie Commission of the 1960s. The *CSIS Act* established a clear mandate for the Service and, for the first time, legislated a framework of democratic control and accountability for a civilian Canadian security intelligence service. In meeting its mandated commitments, CSIS provides advance warning to government departments and agencies about activities which may reasonably be suspected of constituting threats to the country's security. Other departments and agencies, not CSIS, are responsible for taking direct action to counter security threats.

CSIS does not have law enforcement powers, therefore, all law enforcement functions are the responsibility of police authorities. The splitting of functions, combined with comprehensive legislated review mechanisms, ensures that CSIS remains under the close control of the federal government.

In its early years, much of the Service's energy and resources were devoted to countering the spying activities of foreign governments. Time has passed however, and as the world has changed, so has CSIS.

In response to the rise of terrorism worldwide and with the demise of the Cold War, CSIS has made public safety its first

1. This statement is quoted from CSIS's home page: www.csis-scrs.gc.ca/eng/backgrnd/back1_e.html.

priority. This is reflected in the high proportion of resources devoted to counter-terrorism. CSIS has also assigned more of its counter-intelligence resources to investigate the activities of foreign governments that decide to conduct economic espionage in Canada so as to gain an economic advantage or try to acquire technology in Canada that could be used for developing weapons of mass destruction.

Along with these operational changes, CSIS has matured into an organization with a flexible, dynamic structure and, most importantly, an ingrained understanding of its responsibilities and obligations to Canadians. The Service's main purpose is to investigate and report on threats to the security of Canada. This occurs within a framework of accountability to government, as well as respect for the law and the protection of human rights. Nowadays, it also means being more open and transparent to the people it serves. There are some limits on what the Service can discuss; that is the nature of its work, but CSIS is anything but a secret organization.

The Canadian way of life is founded upon a recognition of the rights and freedoms of the individual. CSIS carries out its role of protecting that way of life with respect for those values. To ensure this balanced approach, the *CSIS Act* strictly limits the type of activity that may be investigated, the ways that information can be collected and who may view the information. The *Act* provides many controls to ensure adherence to these conditions.

Information may be gathered, primarily under the authority of section 12 of the *CSIS Act*, only about those individuals or organizations suspected of engaging in one of the following types of activity that threaten the security of Canada, as cited in section 2:

1. Espionage and Sabotage

Espionage: Activities conducted for the purpose of acquiring by unlawful or unauthorized means information or assets relating to sensitive political, economic, scientific or military matters, or for the purpose of their unauthorized communication to a foreign state or foreign political organization.

Sabotage: Activities conducted for the purpose of endangering the safety, security or defence of vital public or private property, such as installations, structures, equipment or systems.

2. Foreign-influenced Activities

Foreign-influenced activities: Activities detrimental to the interests of Canada, and which are directed, controlled, financed or otherwise significantly affected by a foreign state or organization, their agents or others working on their behalf.

For example: Foreign governments or groups which interfere with or direct the affairs of ethnic communities within Canada by pressuring members of those communities. Threats may also be made against relatives living abroad.

3. Political Violence and Terrorism

Threat or acts of serious violence may constitute attempts at compelling the Canadian government to respond in a certain way. Acts of serious violence cause grave bodily harm or death to persons, or serious damage to or the destruction of public or private property, and are contrary to Canadian law or would be if committed in Canada. Hostage-taking, bomb threats and assassination attempts are examples of acts of serious violence that endanger the lives of Canadians. Such actions have been used in an attempt to force particular political responses and change in this country.

Exponents and supporters of political, religious or ideological violence may try to use Canada as a haven or a base from which to plan or facilitate violence in other countries.

Such actions compromise the safety of people living in Canada and the capacity of the Canadian government to conduct its domestic and external affairs.

4. Subversion

Subversion: Activities intended to undermine or overthrow Canada's constitutionally established system of government by violence. Subversive activities seek to interfere with or ultimately destroy the electoral, legislative, executive, administrative or judicial processes or institutions of Canada.

Lawful Protest and Advocacy

The *CSIS Act* prohibits the Service from investigating acts of advocacy, protest or dissent that are conducted lawfully. CSIS may investigate these types of actions only if they are carried out in conjunction with one of the four previously identified types of activity. CSIS is especially sensitive in distinguishing lawful protest and advocacy from potentially subversive actions. Even when an investigation is warranted, it is carried out with careful regard for the civil rights of those whose actions are being investigated.

Security Screening

As well as investigating the four types of threats to Canadian security, CSIS provides security assessments, on request, to all federal departments and agencies with the exception of the Royal Canadian Mounted Police (RCMP), which conducts its own.

These assessments are made with respect to applicants for positions in the Public Service of Canada requiring a security clearance, and for immigration and citizenship applicants.

Security Assessments

The purpose of security assessments is to appraise the loyalty to Canada and reliability, as it relates thereto, of prospective government employees. The intent of the exercise is to determine whether persons being considered for security clearances are susceptible to blackmail or likely to become involved in activities detrimental to national security, as defined in section 2 of the *CSIS Act*. The assessments serve as a basis for recommending that the deputy head of the department or agency concerned grant or deny a security clearance to the individual in question. Security assessments are conducted under the authority of sections 13 and 15 of the *CSIS Act*.

The designated manager in the department or agency determines the security clearance level required for the position to be filled, in accordance with the standards set out in the Government Security Policy. CSIS then conducts the appropriate checks. The duration and depth of the investigation increase with the clearance level.

Immigration and Citizenship

Sections 14 and 15 of the *CSIS Act* authorize the Service to provide security assessments for the review of citizenship and immigration applications to the Department of Citizenship and Immigration.

The assessments provided by the Service for this purpose pertain to the provisions of section 2 of the *CSIS Act* that deal with threats to the security of Canada. The Department of Citizenship and Immigration uses these assessments to review immigration applications in accordance with the inadmissibility criteria set out in the *Immigration and Refugee Protection Act*. On 1 February 1993, this *Act* was amended to include, the terms "terrorism" and "members of an organization." This measure has increased the pertinence of CSIS assessments. Moreover, the inadmissible classes now include, in section 19(1)(f), persons who have engaged, or are members of an organization that has engaged, in acts of terrorism or espionage.

The same practice is followed for citizenship applications. They too are examined on the basis of the definition of threats to the security of Canada set out in section 2 of the *CSIS Act*, and security assessments are provided under section 19 of the *Citizenship Act*.

Questions & Answers

How and when was CSIS created?

CSIS was created by the passage of an Act of Parliament (Bill C-9) on June 21, 1984. The Service began its formal existence on July 16, 1984.

What does CSIS do?

CSIS has a mandate to collect, analyze and retain information or intelligence on activities that may on reasonable grounds be suspected of constituting threats to the security of Canada and in relation thereto, report to and advise the Government of Canada. CSIS also provides security assessments, on request, to all federal departments and agencies, with the exception of the RCMP.

What organization collected security intelligence before CSIS was created?

Prior to June 21, 1984, security intelligence was collected by the Security Service of the RCMP. CSIS was created because the Government of Canada, after intensive review and study, came to the conclusion that security intelligence investigations would be more appropriately handled by a civilian agency. CSIS has no police powers. However, CSIS works with various police forces on those investigations that have both national security and criminal implications. Although CSIS can offer assistance to the police, it has no mandate to conduct criminal investigations.

What constitutes a threat to the security of Canada?

The complete threat definitions can be found in section 2 (a,b,c,d) of the *CSIS Act*. Simply put, terrorism (the planning or use of politically motivated serious violence) and espionage (undeclared foreign intelligence activity in Canada and detrimental to the interests of Canada) are the two major threats which CSIS investigates. Terrorism and espionage can have criminal implications. In such cases, the RCMP investigates and can lay the appropriate criminal charges.

What is "security intelligence" and does the government really need it given that technology allows news broadcasters to deliver information from around the world in a matter of minutes?

Security intelligence is information formulated to assist government decision-makers in developing policy. Regardless of the source of intelligence, it provides value in addition to what can be found in other government reports or in news stories. Intelligence conveys the story behind the story.

How does CSIS obtain this "value-added" component?

The "value-added" comes from analysis and a wide variety of investigative techniques, including the use of covert and intrusive methods such as electronic surveillance and the recruitment and tasking of human sources.

Can these techniques be arbitrarily deployed?

No. All intrusive methods of investigation used by CSIS are subject to several levels of approval before they are deployed. The most intrusive methods—such as electronic surveillance, mail opening and covert searches—require a warrant issued by a judge of the Federal Court of Canada. In addition, the Security Intelligence Review Committee and the Inspector General closely review CSIS operations to ensure they are lawful and comply with the Service's policies and procedures.

What does CSIS do with the security intelligence it collects?

CSIS reports to and advises the Government of Canada. CSIS intelligence is shared with a number of other federal government agencies and departments, including the RCMP and the departments of Foreign Affairs, International Trade, Citizenship and Immigration, and of National Defence. As well, CSIS has arrangements to exchange security-related information with other countries. The vast majority of these arrangements deal with visa vetting. A small number deal with exchanges of information collected by CSIS in its investigation of threats to national security.

What is the difference between a security intelligence service and a foreign intelligence service?

A security intelligence service is restricted to investigating threats to its country's national security. A foreign intelligence service, on the other hand, conducts offensive operations for its government in foreign countries. The methods and objectives of foreign intelligence services differ from country to country.

Does CSIS have any foreign presence at all?

CSIS has liaison offices in some countries. Liaison officers are involved in the exchange of security intelligence information which concerns threats to the security of Canada.

Does CSIS investigate industrial espionage?

CSIS does not investigate company-to-company industrial espionage. CSIS does, however, investigate the activities of foreign governments that engage in economic espionage as a means of gaining an economic advantage for themselves. Economic espionage can be defined as the use of, or facilitation of, illegal, clandestine, coercive or deceptive means by a foreign government or its surrogates to acquire economic intelligence.

What is the impact of foreign government economic espionage activity on businesses in Canada?

Foreign government economic espionage activity exposes Canadian companies to unfair disadvantage, jeopardizing Canadian jobs, Canada's competitiveness and research and development investment.

Does CSIS conduct investigations on university campuses?

CSIS is very sensitive to the special role that academic institutions play in a free and democratic society and the need to preserve the free flow of ideas, therefore, investigations involving university campuses require the approval of senior officials in the Service. Furthermore, human sources and intrusive investigative techniques may only be used with the approval of the Minister for Public Safety and Emergency Preparedness.

Can you name individuals or groups currently under CSIS investigation?

The *CSIS Act* prevents the Service from confirming or denying the existence of specific operations. To disclose such information would impede the Service's investigative capabilities which, in turn, would be injurious to national security. CSIS, however, can assure the public that it is doing everything within its mandate to ensure that Canadians are safeguarded from terrorism and foreign espionage.

Given that the Cold War is over, are there still threats with which Canadians should be concerned?

Yes. Details regarding the Service's view of the security intelligence environment can be found in its annual Public Reports.

Index